aloha

Jam Kali

LIFE AND RACE

THROUGH THE EYES OF A BROWNISH LOCAL GIRL, TITA Ē

By Tracie Keolalani

Print ISBN: 978-1-09832-673-9

eBook ISBN: 978-1-09832-674-6

TABLE OF CONTENTS

Hawaiian Diacritical Marks, ʻokina (glottal stop), and kahakō (macron) are used most of the time in the book. The only instances where the marks are not used are from quotations, authors, or websites that have omitted them.

DEDICATIONS

Na ʻoukou a pau kēia puke, e nā kūpuna, ka ʻohana, nā hoa, a me nā mea i kōkua mai i liʻu mai i ka naʻauao no ka haku ʻana o ia puke nei. A loaʻa ka pono no ka poʻe i hana hewa ʻia ma nēia ʻāina. A hiki i ke aloha ʻāina hope loa. Mahalo

MAHALO, THANKS & ACKNOWLEDGMENTS

All in the ʻohana:

Hoʻoli, Tita, Dad & Mom, Aunty Ninang, and all of you folks (you know who you are)

E Kahiki e project:

- Uncle Kimo Cornwell (musical track)
- Corey Fujimoto (ʻukulele & guitar)
- Michael Grande (mixing, mastering)
- Roke Toʻotoʻo (video concept & videography)
- Hoʻoli (background vocals, video performance)
- Mom (ipu* - Hawaiian percussion instrument and video performance)
- Hiʻilani (video performance)
- Sharnel Kaneshiro (hula, hula choreography)
- Mari Hayes (hula, hula choreography)

Huli ka Naʻau project:

- Kaipoʻi Kelling (song lyrics)
- Kahu Kaleo Patterson (advisor, donation)
- Haʻaheo Guanson (organized donation)
- Mom & Aunty Ninang (advisors)
- Corey Fujimoto (ʻukulele & guitar)
- Mike Grande (mixing, mastering, music track)
- Noah Campbell (introduced me to Bryson)
- Bryson Souza (singing duet)

- Aunty Eileen Hirota (Liliʻuokalani Protestant Church location)
- Tammy Silva (hula choreography, costume)
- Sharnel Kaneshiro (hula)
- Mari Hayes (Hula)
- Carrie & Shane Trinidad (set up & break down location #1)
- Alyssa Young (decorations, set up location #1)
- Sarai Souza (makeup)
- Kili & Chris Haʻo (pictures)
- Roke Tootoo (video & editing)
- Lorelei Kuheana (hair & makeup)

Life and Race Book
- Mom (read/edit)
- Carrie Trinidad (read/input
- Haʻaheo Guanson (read/edit)
- Lorelei Kuheana (photos)
- Jondee Jenss (photo edits, graphics)

TRACIE'S BOOK TRANSLATIONS

- There will be an asterisk* before each word listed in the glossary
- Some definitions are mine and what I understand them to mean
- Footnotes are located at the bottom of each page
- Translation of Hawaiian words will always line up with the official meaning taken from the Hawaiian Dictionary unless otherwise noted
- Each Section has its own glossary
- Each chapter's glossary is located at the end of the chapter.
- The phonetic spelling of words is in ALL-CAPS.
- Hawaiian Vowels are always pronounced the same way:

A = AH, as in "mama"

E = EH, as in "penny"

I = EEY, as in "eat"

O = OH, as in "low"

U = OOH as in "blue"

INTRODUCTION

Aloha everybody. It's me, Tracie. Mahalo* (thanks) for joining me today. Let's start first with my name. Hawaiian names can be difficult to pronounce. Keolalani sounds like this, KEH-OH-LAH-LAH-NEE.

Why did I name this book, "Life and Race Through the Eyes of a Brownish Local Girl,* Tita Ē"? I gave it this name because it is a great description of me and represents who I am. Since this is an autobiography, what better title than one that expresses who I am in my own words.

Why did I write this book? I wrote this because my kūpuna* (ancestors) spoke to me to write this book. I will explain more about kūpuna voices in Chapter 11. I started this book in March 2020 while cooped up at home due to the Covid-19 pandemic. About six months before the pandemic lockdown, I heard the voice of my kūpuna in my "knower," my voice of truth. My knower is the place inside myself that I trust, where I know for sure that I must listen and obey. Other people call that the "voice of God, Holy Spirit, Wise one, Spirit Guide, etc."

In this book, I explain my life and my race. I give you a first-hand view of growing up in Hawai'i. I share my inner struggles and explain the fight within myself to balance living in a colonized Hawai'i under American rule yet fighting to stay true to who I am. I hope to help you see life from my perspective. In doing so hope-fully, it will be a step toward a better understanding and accep-tance of the Hawaiian race and other races.

For the book title, I call myself "brownish." It's not because I don't know what color I am, I AM brown! It's people outside of the Hawaiian Islands who can't seem to label me or figure out what color I am. Here in Hawai'i, we don't refer to ourselves by color, we usually refer to ourselves by ethnicity or blood quantum. And yes, many people born in the islands usually know their blood quantum. When people ask what I am, I tell them it's easy: my dad is 50% Hawaiian and 50% Japanese; my mom is 50% Hawaiian and 50% Filipino; that makes me half of each of their ethnicities, 50% Hawaiian, 25% Japanese, and 25% Filipino. Simple math.

Probably the most common racial stereotypes I hear are, "You don't look Hawaiian, or you look Asian." I find when someone says that to me, I sometimes get irritated. I almost feel like I have to do some kind of song and dance to prove that I am Hawaiian. I can get a little offended, so let me peel away the offense. What do their words mean and what are they trying to say? I understand it because I think the same way sometimes. What they mean is that I don't look like the stereotypical "Hawaiian" person. You know, brown skin, big brown eyes, and dark coarse wavy hair. You've seen the pictures, right? The dark Hawaiian lady dancing with the coconut bra in the fake green plastic hula skirt (btw, that's disgusting to me). It reminds me of the old reruns of Gilligan's Island that I used to watch with their demeaning portrayal of bumbling, stupid, and naïve native people. My skin is brown, but my eyes are almond-shaped, like a cat, my hair is dark, straight, and my face is round. I look like a light caramel-colored Asian lady unless I go out in the sun.

I hear stereotypes about my two daughters' complexion. They both have the same mom and dad, but one is light-colored, and the other is dark-colored. My older daughter, Ho'oli, is Caucasian looking with light brown eyes, light brown straight hair. She is a beautiful fair-skinned woman. My younger daughter, Hi'ilani is Polynesian looking with dark brown eyes, dark brown wavy hair. She is a beautiful dark-skinned tween. Over the years, I've heard comments about their differences. For Ho'oli: "Oh, your daughter is so beautiful, she's so fair-skinned, gorgeous, such a pretty girl;"

For Hiʻilani: "She is dark, she must go to the beach a lot, she looks REAL Hawaiian." For both: "Are they real sisters?"

The thing I love about Hiʻilani is that no matter what anyone says, she sees her beautiful self. She says that her skin is beautiful, and she calls herself the most beautiful one in the family. Once in a while, she asks me, "Mom, do you think I look pretty?" My usual answer is, "What do you think?" She says, "I look pretty." Then I say, "Yep, that's what I think too, you're pretty. What you think of yourself is most important. But make sure you're kind. You can be the prettiest person on the outside, but the ugliest person on the inside. That would mean your real self is ugly."

I would say as a Hawaiian; my color should be brown. But I'm mixed race, so having Japanese blood, I would be considered yellow. I'm also Filipino, so that would be unknown because I don't know what color Filipinos are supposed to represent. To some people, Filipinos are brown and to others they're yellow. So, for my book title, I figured that brown, yellow, and unknown mixed together would be kinda brownish, maybe yellowish-brown or brownish-yellow.

Some of the stories I tell may seem funny, and that is because I tend to add humor to my life experiences after I lived them. I self-reflect and try to do my best to find a laugh in all of my life situations, even the painfully difficult ones. I don't wanna make you sad or angry, I just want to be honest with you. I want you to understand where I've come from, and see the world through my eyes in the life that I've lived. I am mostly optimistic, meaning that I truly believe in the goodness of human beings. I believe that people can change, hopefully for the better after reading my book.

Keep in mind that all the definitions that I present to you are my definitions only. They are not all "official" ones from a dictionary, but they're mine in the way that I understand them and came to know them growing up.

Let us start with the term, "local girl." If you are from the Hawaiian islands or know anything about Hawai'i, it means a girl who was born and raised in Hawai'i. Many from the Continental US and elsewhere are under the impression that if you are from Hawai'i, then you are Hawaiian.

Those folks mistakenly call people from Hawai'i Hawaiians. That seems logical because if you are from California, then you're a Californian, Texas a Texan, and Washington a Washingtonian. However, if you are born and raised in Hawai'i or lived in the islands for a long time you are kama'āina,* LOCAL.

What does it mean to be Hawaiian*? Hawaiian is an ethnicity AND a nationality. It is an ethnicity because there are people, like myself, who have Hawaiian Blood and are of Hawaiian descent. We are Hawaiian.

Who else are Hawaiians? Queen Lili'uokalani was the last reigning queen of Hawai'i. In 1893, the monarchy was overthrown and later was ceded to America illegally. People who were citizens and others who were naturalized before the overthrow were Hawaiian Nationals. Even though the illegal acquisition to America occurred over a hundred years ago, some people with this 'ike* (understanding) do not acknowledge the overthrow. They are Hawaiians. They still consider themselves to be Hawaiian Nationals and part of the Hawaiian Kingdom.

TITA.* Definition 1: (TIH-DAH) This means a female from the islands who may or may not be Hawaiian but is real tough, confrontational, and could give you dirty lickens* (a real beat down). Definition 2: (TEE-TAH) It is a slang word for sister. This is a female who is dear to you. The words are spelled the same but have two different meanings.

TITA Ē.* This tita falls under definition 2. Tita ē is a term of endearment when you call out to a local girl that you regard warmly, pronounced TEE-TAH-EH. That's me!

E komo mai* (welcome) and let me take you on my journey in "Life and Race Through the Eyes of a Brownish Local Girl, Tita Ē."

Glossary of Introduction

1. Mahalo – (MA-HAH-LOH) to be thankful, thanks
2. Local Girl – a female born and raised in Hawai'i or someone who has been living in the islands for a long time
3. Kūpuna – (KOO-POO-NAH) Ancestors, elders (see Chapter 4 for other definition)
4. Kama'āina – a person who is native to Hawai'i, or lived in the islands for a long time,
5. Hawaiian – a person of Hawaiian Descent (Hawaiian blood); a person who is a Hawaiian National, a citizen of the Hawaiian Kingdom
6. 'Ike – (EEH-KAY) knowledge, understanding
7. Tita – 1. (TIH-DAH) a tough chic from Hawai'i; 2. (TEE-TAH) slang for sister
8. Dirty lickens – Pidgin for a real beat down
9. Tita ē – (TEE-TAH-EH) term of endearment for a local girl
10. E komo mai – (EH-KOH-MOH-MA-EE) an idiom for "welcome"

CHAPTER 1

PIDGIN, THE LANGUAGE NOT THE BIRD

Howzit,* how you*? That is Pidgin for "Hi, how are you"? Pidgin,* spoken by some locals is formally known as Hawaiian Pidgin English (aka Hawaiian Creole English and Hawaiian Pidgin). It is used in everyday conversation and has its roots in the old plantation days of Hawai'i. I will use, "talk Pidgin" or "talking Pidgin" rather than "speak Pidgin" or "speaking Pidgin" because that's the way I heard it growing up.

History says that Pidgin originated during the time of the sugarcane plantations. Sometime after 1841, sugarcane was grown and its demand made it a staple production crop for the Hawai'i economy. Large amounts of workers were needed for this labor-intensive crop. However, the Hawaiian population had been destroyed by diseases from foreigners before that time. So immigrants were brought in from all over the world, poor immigrants looking for a better quality of life. Most were Japanese, Chinese, Filipinos, and Portuguese.

These races did not mix but remained in camps separated by their ethnicity. Because they all spoke different languages, they needed a way to communicate with each other. The common language that was born out of that was Pidgin. It is influenced by the languages of the different races, like Japanese, Filipino, and Portuguese but has its foundation in Hawaiian.

The Hawaiian Language was the main language of these islands at that time and was the main way of communicating. So the structure of some Pidgin sentences is apparent. They follow the sentence structure of Hawaiian. For instance, sentence patterns in Pidgin are translated word for word into Hawaiian and vice versa. An example is, "Ugly dat guy (that guy is ugly)" which is "Pupuka kēlā kāne."

Another example is the intonation. English questions end with an upward inflection, Pidgin ends with a downward one. As I listened over the years to mānaleo* (native Hawaiian speakers), the inflection goes high in the middle but goes down at the end of the question. I would laugh as I listened to mānaleo speak because it was funny to hear how the inflections were similar to Pidgin.

Pidgin has a stigma attached to it. "This stigmatization traces back to those sugarcane plantations: Pidgin as broken English for the uneducated immigrant."[1] Attitudes in Hawai'i about it are "it is unamerican, fragmentary, unintelligible."[2] The Hawai'i Board of Education said that it is "lazy, and promotes backward thinking."[3] The media portrays it as, "the language of the unemployed, fun-seeking, teenager, people who are believed to have no serious purpose... not a serious language."[4] Critics say "Pidgin-the local creole language that traces back to Hawaii's plantation era-has no place in the professional world... students need to speak English to get by in life."[5]

---

1 Southwest Magazine https://www.southwestmag.com/pidgin-english/

2 Studyblue https://www.studyblue.com/notes/note/n/hawaiian-creole-english/deck/14436741

3 Ibid #2

4 Ibid #1

5 Civil Beat https://www.civilbeat.org/2013/03/18539-can-or-no-can-pidgin-speakers-in-the-workforce/

Advocate for Pidgin, Lee Tonouchi, who has a master's in English says "that belief is nothing but a product of deep-seated discrimination. And the emphasis on so-called 'standard English,' they say, disregards Hawaii's cultural diversity."[6] Ermile Hargrove, executive director of the Hawai'i Association for Supervision and Curriculum Development and Pidgin advocate explains, "to say you should only have one language is 'restrictive'. Standard English is 'an artificiality that doesn't even exist.'"[7]

The stigma that surrounds Pidgin is similar to the stigma that surrounded the Hawaiian Language. I didn't talk Pidgin much growing up, and I never talked Pidgin in high school. I wanted to fit in with my friends and even though no one told me, Pidgin was spoken at home but was looked down on if I spoke it elsewhere. Maybe that is why I don't remember speaking it in school back from small kid time* (when I was a kid).

I knew that it was looked down upon, and I believed the lie that people who spoke it were supposedly less educated, less cultured, and low income. My family and friends and everyone I knew spoke Pidgin. So, what did it say about me? I should not have believed it, but I did. I am a product of the public school system. The Hawai'i Department of Education was the institution that perpetuated that lie. The lies about Pidgin have been woven into the system, systemic racism.

My first experience having mixed feelings about Pidgin came when I was at my mom's job. It involved my mom's boss' son,

6   Ibid #5

7   Ibid #5

Greg. My mom worked for a prominent attorney, who later became a judge in my hometown. He was a big haole* (Caucasian) man with a very low voice (more explanation about haole in Chapter 3). His nickname was Bud, and I never called him by name. I hardly ever talked to him. I was kind of scared of him at first, but after a while, I started to like him because he would let me stay at work with my mom, and play on her computer. My mom worked from his house and had her office in his garage. I remember going to work with her the whole summer when I was nine years old and playing a typing game all summer long on her computer. Little did I know, it would help me in college to be able to quickly type up my papers.

He had a wife named Mary, and we called her Aunty Mary. Our way in the islands is to call older people "uncle" or "aunty" as a sign of respect. She was a tall haole lady and reminded me of a lady-giant. I don't know why she reminded me of a giant. She was tall but not huge. Maybe it was her hearty laugh. I liked her a lot, and I think she liked me too.

I often observed their two sons. When I met them, their oldest son Stuart was in the 11th or 12th grade in high school. Their younger son Greg was in the 9th grade. At that time, I never had many friends that were haole so I watched them closely. Stuart hardly talked to me. He was very polite, had short dirty blonde hair, but always was busy doing things around the house or going to the beach. He was a pretty tan haole kid, but that's because he was a beach dude. He barely noticed me, but would always come down to my mom's office to talk story* (make small talk) with her. I always wondered why he wanted to talk to my mom all the time, but never to me. It was probably because my mom had a way of showing interest in whatever he had to say, or maybe he had a crush on my attractive mother.

The younger son, Greg seemed peculiar. He was four years older than me and would occasionally let me upstairs into their house to watch TV with him. He gave me snacks, but never let me pick the show. I would look at his white face when he was not looking, and I would always stare at his bright orange hair and freckles. He would talk Pidgin. To me, it always sounded funny. It reminded me of somebody trying to speak a foreign language but never quite did it well enough. He never had the right accent, intonation, or pronunciation. He never stopped trying though.

I was surprised. Here was a haole kid trying to talk Pidgin. I thought that he did it because he wanted to fit in with the locals. But yet here I was, a local girl, who didn't talk Pidgin because I didn't want anyone to look down on me or judge me as dumb and uneducated. It made me feel guilty that Greg was proud to talk Pidgin but couldn't, and I was ashamed to talk Pidgin but could.

As I got older, I didn't see Uncle Bud dem* (them) much. I was a teenager doing my own thing and getting ready for college. My mom would tell me that he always asked how I was doing. He wrote me several letters of recommendation which helped me get scholarships to pay my college tuition. He was always proud that I went away for college to better my life. Looking back, I think I liked him because intuitively, he understood that local people were typically lower-income, and did not usually go for higher education. He always seemed to want to help me make it out of the local rut. The local rut was a trap. Usually, locals would get a job in the tourism industry making peanuts and become slaves to catering to tourists in minimum wage jobs busting their asses just to make ends meet.

Before I left for college I went to my mom's office. Their office had moved to the business district up near Seaview Circle. My mom had her own space with a desk, phone, chair, and all the office stuff. More people were working for Uncle Bud. I sat down and was doing my homework after school near her desk one day. I watched as a local part-Hawaiian, maybe Filipino mixed older man came in. He needed an attorney and he sat near me in the waiting room. He looked uncomfortable. He sat quietly and waited for his name to be called. My mom brought Uncle Bud out and introduced him to the man. The man was still sitting down, and you could tell that he was nervous. He was kind of moving back and forth in his seat but stared straight ahead, no smile. They shook hands and Uncle Bud started making small talk. He was still straight-faced looking intensely at Uncle Bud. My mom broke the ice by joining into the conversation. She started talking Pidgin to the man. Immediately after she started talking Pidgin, the man's body language changed. He relaxed back into his chair, smiled, and loosened up. It was like he knew that everything was going to be ok once he heard my mom. I don't know if my mom realized what had happened, but I did. Pidgin was the unspoken connection between them. Pidgin made everything ok. I don't know what happened to him or if he ended up winning his case. It seemed to me like once he heard Pidgin, he knew he could trust Uncle Bud. Everything was going to be alright.

I had an awkward experience with Pidgin when I went to California to visit my aunty. I was nineteen years old and I went to stay with my mom's sister, her husband, and three kids. One day during my visit, my cousin Toni and her friends were over at the house. There were six of them there, three guys and three girls. She and I are the same age, and her friends were also close in age to us. We were talking about teenage stuff. They were talking about a movie that had recently come out called, "Point Break" starring Patrick Swayze and Keanu Reeves. They were intrigued by the Pidgin in the movie and asked if I would say a couple of words in Pidgin. I felt really stupid, like an animal performing for the crowd in the circus, but I did it anyway. I mumbled a few things and pretended that I was having a conversation with one of my parents. They loved it and kept asking me to say more things and asked for the translations of everyday words.

At the end of this "show," I was embarrassed that I did it, but even amidst the embarrassment, I was proud. I was proud that I was from Hawai'i. I was proud that they appreciated my Pidgin. They clapped and laughed and kept asking me for more, "Say more, tell us more words and Pidgin slangs."

Yet there was this inner nagging in my na'au* (my insides). I thought, "Why do all these haole people appreciate my Pidgin but my own local people look down on it? Why do I look down on it too and feel stupid when my teachers or other Hawai'i people give me condescending looks when I speak it?" I don't know why I never questioned them when people would tell me not to speak it.

These questions and many more would trouble my soul. What deep-seated lies caused me to run away from my Hawaiian-ness growing up? I was ashamed to be Hawaiian. I wished I was haole or hapa-haole* (part Caucasian) so that my skin would be lighter, my eyes not so slanted, and my hair light brown rather than jet black.

As much as I tried to quiet the nagging and the questions, from the beginning of my life as far back as I remember, there was a rumbling. The rumbling felt like the bubbling of hot liquid on fire. I could never turn it off or put it out. It just kept bubbling louder and louder the older I got. It was hot inside my body and made me feel uncomfortable every day. It popped and crackled and caused a constant ringing in my ears. Why couldn't I make it stop?

The only thing that seemed to slow down the bubbling inside me was my mom's words. She told my sister and me that we were Hawaiians. Even though I grew up mixed race, my mom always told us that we were Hawaiians. That was our identity. She always seemed to know that someday, I would embrace it, and come home to my identity. Today, I am proud to be a Hawaiian. I would not want to be anyone else.

Glossary of Chapter 1

1. Howzit – Pidgin for 'hi'
2. How you? – Pidgin for 'how are you'?
3. Pidgin – Hawaiian Creole English
4. Mānaleo – (MA-NAH-LAY-OH) Native Hawaiian Speaker, a person who learned Hawaiian from others who spoke Hawaiian growing up
5. Small Kid Time – Pidgin for hanabata days, the years spent growing up
6. Haole – (HOW-LAY) 1. a Caucasian person; 2. a foreigner not from Hawai'i (more about haole in the Pidgin chapter)
7. Talk story – Pidgin for small talk, shoot the breeze
8. Dem – Pidgin for them, or them guys
9. Na'au – (NAH-OW) insides, guts, inner intuition, feelings
10. Hapa-haole – (HAH-PAH) hapa is an amount meaning a portion or part; a term for a person who is Caucasian mixed with another race (biracial or multiracial)

CHAPTER 2

KA HAMUMU, THE RUMBLING

The dictionary translation describes the word hamumu* as a low indistinct rumbling sound[1]. It reminds me of a volcano. I am not an expert on volcanoes. But, I do know that volcanoes make rumbling noises before they erupt. The sounds are frequencies, below what humans can hear with our naked ears. These sounds occur because of the pressurization of the magma, the hot rock stored in the earth's crust.[2]

In Hawai'i, the volcano is synonymous with the famous Akua* (deity) Pele.* In fact, the Hawaiian word for lava is pele. When the first religious missionaries came to Hawai'i, they were tasked with establishing a written form of the Hawaiian Language. Before that time, Hawaiian was an oral language passed down from generation to generation through oral traditions of songs, chants, and stories.

Missionaries came in 1820, at a time when Hawai'i was riddled with change and unrest. The Hawaiian 'ai kapu* (taboo prohibiting men and women from eating together, or eating certain foods) was abolished, and in doing so, the Hawaiian religious beliefs fell apart. Missionaries saw that as a blessing from God. If

---

1   Wehewehe wikiwiki dictionary https://hilo.hawaii.edu/wehe/

2   Oregon State University, Volcano Sounds http://volcano.oregonstate.edu/book/export/html/385

the Hawaiian religious beliefs were the glue that held life together, then the abolition of it was the bomb that blew it apart.

Hawaiians were spiritual people. Therefore with their religious foundation gone, Christianity filled its place. The view of the supernatural and divine took a new shape in Hawaiʻi. The definition of "God" meant religion and the worship of one God in trinity form; God the Father, God the Son Jesus, and God the Holy Spirit. Missionaries attributed God as the creator of all things.

It is documented that Hawaiians had thousands of "Gods." However, Hawaiians did not necessarily "worship" as the missionaries worshipped. In Hawaiian culture, there are many Akua. Some examples of Akua are: Pele-volcano, creator of ʻāina* (land, earth); Wākea*-space that allows things to grow[3]; Papahānaumoku*-entities that go through regeneration cycles[4]; Kāne*-heat energy and energy that causes evaporation[5]

From an intelligent Hawaiian universal perspective, life-giving forms were Akua, male or female. These Akua were honored and revered because Hawaiians understood that without them, life as we know it would cease to exist. Hawaiians saw Akua in all things.

I never questioned my religion growing up. I was born and raised in Kona, on the island of Hawaiʻi, as a Christian. Our family church for generations was and still is, Lanakila Congregational Church, located in Kainaliu, Hawaiʻi. Many members of my family are buried

---

3 Definition from my notes at Papakū Makawalu Workshop (Edith Kanakaʻole Foundation, February 2020)

4 Definition from my notes at Papakū Makawalu Workshop (Edith Kanakaʻole Foundation January 2020)

5 Ibid #3 and #4

in the church cemetery, including my dad's mom, who I affectionately called Tūtū.

I first recognized the rumbling in college. I was attending UH Mānoa*, on the island of Oʻahu. It was the fall of 1992, the last semester before I graduated with my Bachelor's in International Business. I took my first Hawaiian language class. It was at a night school class for adults held at Kaimukī High School. My teacher was a woman named Nohealani. I was a little scared and intimidated by her, so I never talked to her or spoke up. She told stories of Hawaiian history and incorporated those stories into the language lessons. I could not believe that nobody ever taught me the true history of Hawaiʻi. I did not learn it, not in elementary, intermediate, or high school. I didn't even learn it in college. I had to learn it at this no credit night school class.

I felt the rumbling as it moved around inside of me. I realized that I felt it since I was a little girl. It's the feeling of strange emotions moving around inside my naʻau whenever something was not quite right. It was sometimes "chicken skin*" (skin tingling sensation) that made the hairs on my arms and the back of my neck stand up. It was the angry, frustrated, and righteous flame that would heat up inside me whenever I saw or experienced injustice happening.

I flew home several weeks later and told my parents that I was quitting being a Christian. I could not be a part of a religion that was associated with the ruin and near extinction of my people and language. I hated these people who professed God, yet caused so much pain, and destruction to my homeland. My parents were distraught.

The very next night after I came home, I was sitting in the sanctuary of Lanakila Church. My parents were sitting on one side, I was on the opposite side, and Kahu* (pastor) Adams was sitting in the middle. He was the kahu of Lanakila since I had been a young girl.

Kahu had retired from his job somewhere in the Continental US. He and his wife who we called Mama Kahu* (pastor mom) moved to Kona to live out their retirement years. In doing so, he took the job as Kahu of my church. They were really old haole people. They were nice to me, but I always felt like they did not understand us, locals. I did not feel comfortable around them. I cannot explain why... maybe it's because even after all the years that they lived in Hawai'i, they could not pronounce Hawaiian words or names correctly. I laughed every time they said Hawaiian words and butchered them. Even after so many years of living in Kona, their pronunciation never got better.

That night, kahu sat staring at me. He kept looking back and forth between my parents and me. I felt a little weird, but I did not care what any of them had to say. Nothing would change my mind because I had already made it up. He showed me Bible scriptures and read them to me. To this day, I don't remember anything he said. I only remember him praying for me and for my relationship with God and my family. I didn't change my stance, but I told them that I would remain open to allow Akua to bring me revelation in my spiritual life. It brought me peace and comfort. I continue to allow Akua to lead me in my daily walk of life.

I consider myself a Christian. I believe in Akua and am very spiritual. I also believe that I am guided by my 'aumākua* (family guardians) and my kūpuna. I have faith in knowing my truth and my way to God. Every religion has some truth. This is my way of amalgamating the traditional Hawaiian religion with Christianity.

Even though I believe in God, I still have hesitations about religion. It was the missionaries who translated the Bible from English to Hawaiian to convert Hawaiians to Christianity. It was them, the descendants of missionaries who overthrew my queen while lining their pockets and becoming extremely wealthy in the process. I struggle with the belief system brought to us by them, the haole.

Glossary of Chapter 2

1. Hamumu – (HAH-MOO-MOO) A low indistinct rumbling sound; an indistinct sound of conversation[6]

2. Akua[7] – (AH-KOO-AH) god/gods [singular/plural], goddess, spirit, ghost, image, idol, corpse, divine, supernatural, godly; among Hawaiians formerly, the name of any supernatural being, the object of fear or worship, a god.

3. Pele – (PEH-LAY) Ka wahine ʻai honua (the earth eating woman), Goddess of Volcano, also known as Madame Pele, or Tūtū Pele; lava flow, volcano, eruption, kūpuna to Hawaiians

4. ʻAi Kapu – (AYE-KAH-POO) Restrictions on eating (ie. Men & women were not allowed to eat certain foods, not allowed to eat together, etc.)

5. ʻĀina – (AYE-NAH) land, earth

6. Wākea – (WAH-KEH-AH) Sky Father, ancestor of all Hawaiians, space that allows things to grow

7. Papahānaumoku – (PAH-PAH-HAH-NOW-MOH-KOO) Earth mother, ancestor of all Hawaiians/entities that go through regeneration cycles on land and in the sea

8. Kāne – (KAH-NAY) Name of a Hawaiian God, representing certain aspects of water

9. UH Mānoa – (MA-NO-AH) University of Hawaiʻi at Mānoa

---

6 Andrews Hawaiian/English Dictionary https://hilo.hawaii.edu/wehe/?q=hamumu

7 The Office of Hawaiian Education Definition (part of the Hawaiʻi Department of Education)

10. Chicken skin – Pidgin for goosebumps, or skin tingling sensations that can be attributed to a positive or a negative experience

11. Kahu – (KAH-HOO) Pastor, minister, or priest

12. Mama Kahu – (MA-MA-KAH-HOO) Wife of the pastor, Pastor Mom

13. 'Aumākua[1] – (OW-MA-KOO-AH) family or personal gods, deified ancestors who might assume the shape of sharks, owls, hawks, mudhens, octopuses, eels, mice, rats, dogs, caterpillars, rocks, cowries, clouds, or plants. A symbiotic relationship existed; mortals did not harm or eat 'aumākua, and 'aumākua warned and reprimanded mortals in dreams, visions, and calls.

---

1   Wehewehe wikiwiki https://hilo.hawaii.edu/wehe/?q=aumakua

CHAPTER 3

HAOLE; CAUCASIANS, FOREIGNERS, OR BOTH

Haole* is a tricky word. It has several meanings. Growing up, I only knew one meaning #1 – a white or Caucasian person. Most of the time when people talk about "haoles" they mean Caucasian. By the way (side note) in Hawaiian, the plural for haole is haole (the English language adds an "s" at the end of a word to make it plural, i.e.: girl/girls, boy/boys). The second meaning is #2 – a foreigner. The dictionary defines haole as: "a person with white skin, hence a foreigner. But Hawaiians say haole eleele for negro; a person from a foreign country; an alien, especially one of Anglo-Saxon stock (the foreigners who arrived first in the islands were white persons)."[2] When I talk about haole in the book, I will notate whether I mean #1 a Caucasian, #2 a foreigner, or #1 & #2 for both.

I have heard other people translate the word haole as "hā-'ole*" meaning no breath, or without breath. I cannot confirm the validity of this story, but my friend told me that when foreigners came and greeted native people, they reached out to shake hands. Native people's usual greeting with other natives is a honi* (traditional kiss, touching noses). A honi was symbolic in that when two people touched noses, they were honoring each other and sharing

---

2 Wehewehe Wikiwiki https://hilo.hawaii.edu/wehe/?q=haole

the breath of life. Because those haole (def#2) people did not honi, or share breath, it meant that they were breath-less, or hā-ʻole.

Haole has a stigma to it. Many haole (def#1) who come to Hawaiʻi or move to Hawaiʻi have been called haole in a pejorative way. Some Caucasians have told me that they felt like haole was a bad word, similar to the n-word for Blacks. I remind them that haole does NOT mean the n-word for Caucasians. It is all in the way it is used.

The way the word haole is used in a sentence will define its intent. "Mom, me and my friend Carrie are coming over for dinner tonight. You remember her? You met her before, my haole friend from Mililani," would be a factual statement. If my intention was negative and I said, "Eh, you effen haole, what you doing in Hawaiʻi? Go back to where you came from," that would be offensive. It all comes down to the meaning and use.

I am not going to lie, I get angry at haole (def#1 & #2) people sometimes. I don't like it when I get angry just because of somebody's skin color. I sometimes judge a person based on the way they look. Given the history of the overthrow, I sometimes feel justified when I get angry. I don't want to act in a racist manner so I have to regularly check myself and talk to myself. When I have crappy thoughts about white people, I try to listen to my words to make sure I stay in control over my emotions and behavior. I try to quickly cast down those "judgy" thoughts to keep my attitude in check. It's not always easy.

The other night, my mom had to put me back in check. We were eating dinner together and we had some leftovers. I opened up the foil on the leftover plates and put out the fish, beef tripe stew, and rice. My mom took out the coleslaw that my sister brought over the night before. I said, "Ugh, coleslaw. That's the white man's food." My mom snapped at me, "you know this is all white man's food. You need to watch what you say because the kids hear you. That's racist. I don't want them to talk like that." I didn't mean it in a racist way. I just meant that local people don't usually eat coleslaw unless it's with KFC chicken, biscuits, and gravy. Coleslaw is haole (def#2) food to me. That was an offensive statement and my mom made me realize it.

Later that night, we were talking about Liliʻuokalani and the overthrow of the Hawaiian kingdom. I asked my mom to borrow her book, "Hawaii's Story by Hawaii's Queen." My sister asked what it was about, and I said, "It's Liliʻuokalani telling her story of her life and the events of the overthrow. She writes about how her advisors betrayed her, imprisoned her in her own home, stole the kingdom, took the land, and stripped away her title and wealth." My mom said, "I don't want to read that book. It's sad. I feel so much sympathy for what happened to her." Then I said, "Yah mom. That's why sometimes I feel angry and make statements about haole (def#1 & 2) people. I hate what they did to my queen." It's not right what I say out of anger sometimes. I DO stereotype people and I know that I do it. I try to be aware of it so I can do better the next time."

I am an intermediate/high school Hawaiian language and music teacher. In teaching, I always weave in the overthrow. We discuss how Hawaiians adapted to the pain of living in a colonized Hawaiʻi after that monumental time in history. Most kids today know the history of the overthrow as compared to previous generations like mine in the 80s who were brainwashed to accept and embrace the "white" perspective of history. The word haole (def#1 & #2) always comes up.

It can get uncomfortable. I do my best to talk openly, be open-minded, and have open dialogue as we go through steps to make sure to respect each other and each person's opinion. Some kids open up and tell their personal stories about it. Some kids hate the word and give their reasons for hating it. Others don't think much of it and use it to describe Caucasians. Somebody will always ask, "Kumu* (the name that my students call me, which means teacher), do you like haoles (def#1 & #2)?" I had a student say, "I hate haoles (def#1), do you? You do right, Kumu? Right? THEY STOLE OUR LAND!"

I get a lot of hard questions as a kumu. I sometimes answer hard questions with stories. I giggle because every time I say, "Lemme tell you a story," the kids sigh. Sometimes it's a long story. It always has a life lesson wrapped up inside of it like laulau* (a food dish made usually with meat like beef, chicken, or butterfish wrapped inside of taro leaves, sealed with a lāī* (ti-leaf) package, and tied tightly with a small piece of string).

I tell them this story. My two daughters are part haole (def#1) on their dad's side. They are part-German. On my side of the family, when Japanese and Filipinos came to work on the plantations in Hawai'i a long time ago, some of them were my 'ohana* (family). My 'ohana were plantation workers. I am part-Japanese and part-Filipino. My people were haole (def#2) when they first arrived here. So if I hated foreigners wouldn't I be hating my kids, myself, and the people in my 'ohana?

I ask them about Hawaiian culture and Hawaiian values. I ask if they think continuing those things are important. They always say "yes." I ask them to give examples of Hawaiian values. They say things like mālama ʻāina* (caring for land), respecting Hawaiian religious beliefs, Hawaiian customs, and language. I tell them that I learned to speak Hawaiian in college. My kumu, Kumu Puhi is haole (def#1), and he taught me to speak Hawaiian. I say, "He is a haole (def#1) white man who is perpetuating the language. Is it ok that a haole (def#1) taught me the language of my ancestors?"

That leads right into the Hawaiian Mindset, or the Hawaiian perspective and way of thinking (explained in Chapter 6). That always opens up more discussions with students. By the end of the discussions, they usually have more questions. Most times, the dialogue makes the students and myself more aware of our thoughts, feelings, and beliefs. To me, awareness is key.

Glossary of Chapter 3

1. Haole – (HOW-LAY) def#1 a white or Caucasian person; def#2 a foreigner

2. Hā – (HAH) breath

3. ʻOle – (OH-LAY) without or not

4. Honi/hongi – (HOE-NEE) means a kiss, a traditional honi is a greeting between two people touching noses

5. Kumu – (KOO_MOO) teacher

6. Laulau – (LAH-OOH-LAH-OOH) Hawaiian food dish usually made with meat or starch wrapped in taro leaves, sealed in a ti-leaf wrapper, and tied with string

7. Lāī – (LAH-EEY) ti-leaf, a very important plant to native Hawaiians used for medicinal, religious, and other functional purposes

8. ʻOhana – (OH-HAH-NAH) family, extended family

9. Mālama ʻāina – (MA-LAH-MA-AH-EEY-NAH) caring for the land, respect for the earth and all aspects of nature (wildlife, sea life, plants, etc.)

CHAPTER 4

I MUA, I HOPE; THE FUTURE AND THE PAST

At the turn of the century, Hawaiian was still the main language of native people. The provisional government, led by Sanford B. Dole, the son of Protestant missionaries to Hawai'i, knew that they had to decrease 'ōlelo Hawai'i so that English could flourish. In 1896, just 3 years after the illegal overthrow, a law was passed that banned the use of the Hawaiian language in the public and private school system. Teachers were told that speaking Hawaiian with children would result in job termination. Children were harshly punished for speaking Hawaiian in school.[1] The law stated:[2]

The English Language shall be the medium and basis of instruction in all public and private schools, provided that where it is desired that another language shall be taught in addition to the English language, such instruction may be authorized by the Department, either by its rules, the curriculum of the school, or by direct order in any particular instance. Any schools that shall not conform to the provisions of this section shall not be recognized by the Department.

---

1   'Aha Pūnana Leo www.ahapunanaleo.org/index.php?/about/history/
2   US Congress 1898, The Laws of Hawaii, Ch.10, Section 123

Hawaiians were proud of their heritage, culture, and language. It was an oral language before the coming of the missionaries. Hawaiian history continued to be passed down from generation to generation. They had the kuleana* (responsibility) to transmit the information accurately. They knew their moʻokūʻauhau* (genealogy) since the beginning of creation. The kumulipo* (a Hawaiian Creation Chant) consisted of over 2,000 lines, all of which were held in the memory of Hawaiians and passed on until it eventually made its way onto written paper.

There was a saying that angered me. My kumu in Hawaiian class said that this was a strategy used by the government. They said, "if we can get rid of the language, then we can get rid of the people."[3] That was the plan of the rebels who stole Hawaiʻi. They cut the language off from children to stop the perpetuation. They punished the children, tried to beat the language out of them, and humiliated them so they would feel ashamed of being Hawaiian. They tried to erase our history, so we would forget who we were as native people. That's how they almost killed the ʻōlelo Hawaiʻi.

The Hawaiian word for the past or before is "ma mua" or "i mua.*" Yet "i mua" also means to move forward. The Hawaiian word for the future or afterward is "ma hope" or "i hope." Yet "i hope*" also means behind.

My understanding is that you cannot walk into the future without seeing what is behind you. That means that Hawaiians understood that the future was always to move forward while facing what was behind. History tells us that it tends to repeat itself. I am reminded of the quote that says, "Those who do not learn from history are condemned to repeat it."[4]

---

3 Quote by an unknown author

4 Quote credited to philosopher George Santayana

As I continued in the ʻōlelo Hawaiʻi* (Hawaiian Language) classes with Nohealani, the rumbling got louder. It was like my naʻau was starting to heat up. I felt like something was moving and shaking inside of me. I wondered if it was because I was uncomfortable being a part-Hawaiian girl, not sure of who I was, and what I stood for. I wondered if it was because I was ashamed of my ancestry.

I realized that I could not move forward without knowing my past, the real past. Not the past that was taught to me through books that perpetuated the racist attitudes and viewpoints of the colonizer. I was scared of learning about my people and their painful past. I was scared because learning these things made me angry. I was heating up inside and getting madder.

I was searching for the answers. I knew that ʻōlelo Hawaiʻi would lead me to those answers. I asked my family why they did not speak Hawaiian. Both sets of grandparents were born around the 1920s. Both my momʻs mom and my dadʻs mom spoke Hawaiian as their primary language. They were mānaleo but their kids could not ʻōlelo* (speak). I kept asking my family why not.

My mom told me that her mom, Grandma Frances, spoke Hawaiian to them. My mom was the second to the youngest of eleven kids. She remembers how her older brothers got beaten in school by their teachers for speaking Hawaiian. Those were common stories in the Hawaiian community back in the old days. Teachers would go to houses and tell parents not to speak to their kids in Hawaiian, or else they would get punished and beaten up in school. This was about 50 years after the law was passed, and they were still suffering the consequences of that law.

My mom said that it was partly her fault that she didn't speak Hawaiian growing up. Grandma Frances spoke to her and her siblings, but she was not interested in her mom's language, and the "old" Hawaiian ways. She said that she sometimes put her mom down, and made her feel stupid. She would tell her mom that Hawaiian was not what they were learning in school. It wasn't all her fault. It was the system of institutional racism toward our people that brainwashed her.

My dad's story is a little different. I spent a lot of time with his mom, Lottie. I called her Tūtū* (grandparent). My impression back then was that she was ashamed of Hawaiian. I felt that way because she never spoke in Hawaiian to anyone except her 'ohana and friends who were mānaleo. I would go to her house and hear her laughing and talking story in the kitchen. I stayed outside or in the parlor (living room) of the house playing with my toys and would hear them 'ōlelo. As a little kid, I would try to hang out with them but a lot of times they wouldn't let me. It was the old days when kids were to be seen, but not heard. Nowadays, I still enjoy being in the company of kūpuna* (old people, grandparents) and listening to their stories.

I used to sit in the hallway, right outside of the kitchen. It was only an ear's distance away so I would listen to them wala'au* (talk story). I remember them sitting, talking, and laughing together for hours speaking in Hawaiian. I never understood most of what they were saying but I sat and listened whenever I could. I loved listening to them. They sounded so happy.

I knew that I shouldn't go into the kitchen, because whenever I did, they would all straighten up and stop their 'ōlelo Hawai'i chit chat. It kind of felt like I had caught them doing something wrong. Their English was mostly Pidgin, but I still saw them stiffen up when a non-Hawaiian speaker came in. To me, it was like they were hiding a part of themselves. They were hiding their ʻōlelo. It was the part of themselves that they loved to express but wouldn't share with the rest of us. It seemed like they felt afraid that we would be subjected to the kind of abuse that they experienced for being carriers of their ʻōlelo makuahine* (mother tongue). Tūtū never shared her language with her husband, my grandpa Teruo, a second-generation Hawaiʻi born pure Japanese man. He spoke English and a little bit of broken Japanese. She didn't share her gift, maybe because she didn't see it as a gift. Nobody got the benefit of carrying it to the next generation, not her husband, her kids, or her grandkids.

I was angry but did not want my anger to be misdirected. I remember when I was young, some people talked about "kill haole*" (def#1) days. Those were days when kids went to school or went out into the community to make trouble or beat up anybody that looked haole (def#1), or white, even tourists. I never experienced it firsthand or knew of anyone personally that went out looking to "kill haole" (def#1) on any specific day. It may have been true, but it was wrong. That was ignorant behavior. Not only was it foolish, but it was also dangerous and resulted in spewing hate, not aloha* (love).

Aloha means love! Love is always the answer. It sounds cliché but I was on a mission. I needed to learn the ʻōlelo makuahine. I loved it. I embraced it. I was proud of my ʻōlelo. To move forward into the future, I needed to learn the language of my past. I had to make sure that the language lived on. I needed to teach it to my children (which I didn't have at the time) and to the future generations. I would teach them history, the REAL history, so they could carry it proudly. Eō* (the answer to a call)!

Glossary of Chapter 4

1. Kuleana – (KOO-LAY-AH-NAH) responsibility, privilege
2. Moʻokūʻauhau – (MOW-OH-KOO-OW-HOW) genealogy, family tree
3. Kumulipo – (KOO-MOO-LEE-POE) Hawaiian creation chant starting from the beginning until today
4. I mua – (EEY-MOO-AH) before or to move forward
5. I hope – (EEY-HOE-PAY) after or to move backward
6. ʻŌlelo Hawaiʻi – (OH-LAY-LOW-HAH-WHY-EEY) Hawaiian Language
7. ʻŌlelo – (OH-LAY-LOW) language; to speak
8. Tūtū – (TOO-TOO) grandparent
9. Kupuna/kūpuna – (KOO-POO-NAH) grandparent, old person [singular]/Kūpuna [plural] (see Introduction for other definition)
10. Walaʻau – (WAH-LAH-OW) talk story, shoot the breeze
11. ʻŌlelo Makuahine – (OH-LAY-LOW-MA-KOO-AH-HEE-NAY) mother tongue, the Hawaiian language
12. Kill haole days – days when locals would go out looking for haole (def#1) people and beat them up, just because they looked foreign or like they weren't from Hawaiʻi
13. Aloha – (AH-LOW-HAH) love, gratitude, kindness, sympathy
14. Eō – (EH-OH) yes, I am here, the answer to a call

CHAPTER 5

KŪʻĒ; CIVIL RESISTANCE VERSUS CIVIL DISOBEDIENCE

The definition of kūʻē* means to oppose, resist, or protest. After the overthrow, Hawaiians channeled their kūʻē toward the new government and their love for the queen through their mother tongue.

Language is the pocket that holds our culture. Without our language, then who are we, and with whom do we identify? Hawaiians understood that. There were over a hundred Hawaiian language newspapers during the period surrounding the overthrow. Hawaiians saw their language diminishing right before their eyes. They watched English dominate and become the main language. The way to kūʻē was to write down the Hawaiian words, stories, values, mindsets, ideas, feelings, and beliefs so they would not disappear.

They wrote mele* (songs, chants), moʻolelo* (stories, usually true or factual), kaʻao* (fables, usually made up or embellished), and their manaʻo* (thoughts, ideas) down in those newspapers. One such mele, famous for its defiance to the new government is "Kaulana Nā Pua" also known as "Mele ʻAi Pōhaku:"[1]

---

1 Huapala.org https://www.huapala.org/Kau/Kaulana_Na_Pua.html

Kaulana Nā Pua	Famous are the Children
Kaulana nā pua a'o Hawai'i	Famous are the children of Hawai'i
Kūpa'a ma hope o ka 'āina	Ever loyal to the land
Hiki mai ka 'elele o ka loko 'ino	When the evil-hearted messenger comes
Palapala 'ānunu me ka pākaha	With his greedy document of extortion
Pane mai Hawai'i moku o Keawe	Hawai'i, land of Keawe answers
Kōkua nā Hono a'o Pi'ilani	Pi'ilani's bays help
Kāko'o mai Kaua'i o Mano	Mano's Kaua'i lends support
Pa'apū me ke one Kākuhihewa	And so do the sands of Kākuhihewa
'A'ole a'e kau i ka pūlima	No one will fix a signature
Ma luna o ka pepa o ka 'enemi	To the paper of the enemy
Ho'ohui 'āina kū'ai hewa	With its sin of annexation
I ka pono sivila a'o ke kanaka	And sale of native civil rights
'A'ole mākou a'e minamina	We do not value
I ka pu'u kālā o ke aupuni	The government's sums of money
Ua lawa mākou i ka pōhaku	We are satisfied with the stones
I ka 'ai kamaha'o o ka 'āina	Astonishing food of the land
Ma hope mākou o Lili'ulani	We back Lili'ulani

A loaʻa ē ka pono o ka ʻāina	Who has won the rights of the land
*(A kau hou ʻia e ke kalaunu)	*(She will be crowned again)
Haʻina ʻia mai ana ka puana	Tell the story
Ka poʻe i aloha i ka ʻāina	Of the people who love their land

*Alternate Stanza

By Ellen Kehoʻohiwaokalani Wright Prendergast

Source: Na Mele o Hawaiʻi Nei by Elbert & Mahoe – written Jan. 1893, published in 1895, this himeni opposed the annexation of Hawaiʻi to the United States. The original title was Mele ʻAi Pohaku or The Stone-eating Song, and was also known as Mele Aloha ʻĀina or the Patriot's song. This song was composed as Ellen Wright Prendergast was sitting in the garden of her father's house in Kapālama. Members of the Royal Hawaiian Band visited her and voiced their unhappiness at the takeover of the Hawaiian Kingdom. They begged her to put their feelings of rebellion to music.

The word kūʻē does not differentiate whether civil resistance or civil disobedience is closer to its meaning. What is the difference between civil resistance and civil disobedience? Civil disobedience[2] is defined as, "the refusal to obey the demands or commands of a government or occupying power, without resorting to violence or active measure of opposition; its usual purpose is to force concessions from the government or occupying power."

Civil resistance[3], "also referred to as nonviolent action, nonviolent struggle, nonviolent conflict, and people power, is

---

2   Encyclopedia Brittanica https://www.britannica.com/topic/civil-disobedience

3   Oxford Bibliographies https://www.oxfordbibliographies.com/view/document/obo-9780199743292/obo-9780199743292-0194.xml

a technique for waging conflict for political, economic, and/or social objectives without threats or use of physical violence... By this definition, civil resistance is a technique of struggle employing methods outside traditional institutional channels for making change in a society. Many civil resisters, however, engage in both institutional processes for making change while also waging civil resistance to bring exogenous pressure on a political, economic, or social system."

The definition of disobedience[4] is, "refusing to do what someone in authority tells you to do." So the question then becomes, is disobeying an unjust law or an immoral rule considered disobedience? The Jim Crow laws[5] were "state and local laws that enforced racial segregation in the Southern United States... The laws were enforced until 1965."

Rosa Parks' refusal to move to the back of a bus because she was black and Dr. Martin Luther King, Jr's peaceful civil rights movement, by definition were considered "disobedience." Yet what would life be like today if brave people of the past never resisted unjust laws? I disagree with the definition of civil disobedience. I would argue that one cannot be disobedient to an unjust or immoral authority figure, rule, or law because there is no true authority without justice.

---

4   Cambridge Dictionary https://dictionary.cambridge.org/us/dictionary/english/disobedience

5   Wikipedia https://en.wikipedia.org/wiki/Jim_Crow_laws

I remember watching the movie "Roots" when I was a young girl. It freaked me out to see all the haole (def#1) people hunt down Kunta Kinte and the other Africans. I cried when they were caught in the nets. "They stole Kunta Kinte, they stole Kunta Kinte," I said. I recently watched it again. This time, I thought about their history back in Africa, especially their ʻōlelo. How long did it take for all the Kunta Kintes to forget their ʻōlelo? How long did it take for them to lose their mother tongue? Did they have anyone to speak it to? Did they teach it to their kids? It made me mad. Their language, customs, and history got erased just like the Hawaiians.

The struggle to keep the ʻōlelo alive is one I think of daily. There is not one day that I don't think about its impact and consequences. What would have happened if my ʻōlelo had died? What would happen if, in the future, it were to weaken and die?

When I was a kid, I thought Tūtū had been hiding her ʻōlelo. But as I grew up, I looked at her actions from another viewpoint. I now believe that she was practicing civil resistance. I realized that she was not hiding it, but protecting it. She refused to stop speaking it. Even though she had been punished growing up for speaking it, she never stopped. Kūʻē.

I only knew Tūtū as my sweet, soft-spoken grandma. When I became an adult, I learned that she was tough, a tita (def #1) on the inside with spunk. I heard stories about her no-nonsense attitude. She could be fiery when she wanted to be. Tūtū had already passed away, but Aunty Koko, my dad's oldest sister told me a story about Tūtū. She said that she was almost aborted when Tūtū was pregnant with her. She was proud when she told that story. She would say, "yep, I'm still alive because of my mom." She retold the story at least a couple of times a year with a big smile on her face.

It started like this. It was 1947 when interracial relations were not commonplace in the islands. My grandpa, Teruo was a nisei* (second-generation Japanese American) born to pure Japanese parents on the Big Island. Grandpa had married Tūtū, a pure Hawaiian woman. At the time, they were a young couple in their 20s that had fallen in love. They got married and Tūtū got pregnant. Grandpa's mom and one of his sisters did not approve of the relationship. When they found out that Tūtū was pregnant, they tried to convince her to get rid of it. The child would be a half breed, born half-Japanese, and half-Hawaiian. They repeatedly told her to abort the child, but she refused to do so. I cannot imagine what kind of feelings she had inside knowing that her in-laws wanted her to kill her unborn child. Years later, my dad told me that eventually, they came to love and accept her. But if she hadn't stood up to them, Aunty Koko would have never been born. Kū'ē.

My mom demonstrates kū'ē to me through her words, actions, and behavior all the time. I was afraid of adults growing up, especially haole (def#1 & #2) people. I don't know why. I didn't answer back. Respect for older people, especially kūpuna is a value that is ingrained in most local kids from a very young age. Once when I was nine years old, we were on vacation in Nevada. While in our hotel room, she asked me to make a collect call to our family back home in Hawai'i. Those were the 70s, at a time when there were no cell phones. It was a big black phone with a long black curly cord that connected to a receiver with numbers and a rotary dial. It weighed about two pounds and sat on top of a desk.

I dialed 0 on the phone and waited for the operator to answer. In those days, you couldn't call someone directly in another state. You had to call the operator, give her the number you were trying to reach, and she would connect you to that person. Long-distance calls were not free. My mom told me to make a collect call. I was a little nervous, but my mom always made me do grown-up things like talk to adults, so it didn't scare me. In my loudest kid voice,

I asked the operator if I could make a collect call. I could tell by her voice that she was a haole (def#2) lady. She started to ask me questions like, "Where are your parents. Why are you using the phone? Are you making a prank call?" She didn't give me time to think of the answers. She just kept quizzing me. When I didn't answer, she started yelling at me. I was trying to answer her, but I couldn't get words out. I started crying. My mom grabbed the phone away. She was pissed. I heard her say, "That is MY daughter. I gave her permission to use the phone. I asked her to make that collect call. She was not fooling around on the phone. She was making a collect call to get in touch with our family in Hawai'i. You owe my daughter an apology." She handed me back the phone. The lady sounded shook up and said, "I'm sorry. What number are you trying to reach?" I told her the number and she connected me.

I learned a very valuable lesson that day. My mom was not rude or mean to the lady on the phone, she was firm. She taught me that when I am right, then I need to speak out to protect my rights. It was my job to stand up for myself, even when I feel scared. I also learned that when someone else is right I need to speak out to protect their rights, especially if they are too afraid or intimidated to do so for themselves. I don't remember much else about that call. I don't remember the conversation with my aunty once the operator connected me. One thing I remember most from that day, I stood up straighter and taller. Kū'ē.

Glossary of Chapter 5

1. Kū'ē – (KOO-EY) to oppose or resist, to go against
2. Mele – (MEH-LAY) song, chant, poem
3. Mo'olelo – MOH-OH-LEH-LOW) story (usually true)
4. Ka'ao – (KAH-OW) story (usually a fable)

5. Mana'o – (MA-NAH-OH) ideas, thoughts (see Chapter 11 for other definition)
6. Nisei – Japanese word for second-generation Japanese American

CHAPTER 6

E OLA MAU KA ʻŌLELO HAWAIʻI, THE HAWAIIAN LANGUAGE LIVES

E ola mau ka ʻōlelo Hawaiʻi* means the Hawaiian language lives, or lives on.

I gave examples of the abuse that my ʻohana experienced when speaking their ʻōlelo. As the Hawaiian language declined, one devastating result was the loss of what I call, the "Hawaiian Mindset."* Wikipedia defines the word mindset as, "a set of assumptions, methods, or notations held by one or more people or groups of people. A mindset can also be seen as arising out of a person's worldview or philosophy of life.[1]" I credit the Hawaiian Mindset definition to my friend and fellow kumu, Kaipoʻi Kelling. [2]

I created a wikiō* (video) and asked Kaipoʻi to help explain these events. I wanted people to understand the repercussions of ripping away the home language* from the people. One thing he shared that resonated with me was an ʻōlelo noʻeau* (Hawaiian proverb). It says, "I ka ʻōlelo nō ke ola, i ka ʻōlelo nō ka make."[3] He

---

1   Wikipedia https://en.wikipedia.org/wiki/Mindset

2   YouTube "Why Hawaiian is not the main language of Hawaii, Kaipoʻi Kelling" https://www.youtube.com/watch?v=v7rWe78J5iA

3   Pūkuʻi, ʻŌlelo Noʻeau 1191

translates it as, "In life there is language, and in death, there is language too," He points out that what is most valuable about 'ōlelo Hawai'i is the Hawaiian thought and thinking process. When the Hawaiian Language is lost by people not speaking Hawaiian, then the no'ono'o Hawai'i* (Hawaiian thought process), or the Hawaiian mindset is lost too. The result is death. It works in reverse too when people keep speaking it. The result is life.

After I graduated from college with my business degree, I immediately got hired. My old boss at the university, where I worked as a student assistant, hooked me up with one of her friends in another department. I foolishly went on a spending spree, buying a brand new Honda Civic, electronics, bags, shoes, and party clothes for the weekends. It was the first time that I had money. I was rich.

It was 1993, and I was back on the UH campus working at my new job. It was like I never left. I got to see my friends and hang out with them. I got hired full-time at UH's personnel department. I processed paperwork helping foreign teachers and professors from other countries get visas to come to Hawai'i and work at my university.

In a few short months, I started to hate that job. I was bored, I didn't like the work, and I couldn't stand my boss, Amy. She was pushy and sassy, but I sucked at that job too. I wasn't cut out to do paperwork and sit at a desk all day. I wanted to tell Amy to take that job and shove it, but I was in so much debt that I needed the money.

I was trying to figure out how I could go back to college and get a Hawaiian degree so I could work in a job, any job, with ʻōlelo Hawaiʻi. The night class with Kumu Nohealani ended, but my goal was to become a fluent speaker. I didn't have any friends who could ʻōlelo, so I bought a book called "Ka Lei Haʻaheo." That's the book the first year Hawaiian students used at UH.[4]

By that time, both Tūtū Lottie and Grandma Frances had passed on. It was the 90s, the Blockbuster Video generation. There was no internet, so I had to teach myself Hawaiian. I read the chapters of the book, did the written work, and practiced saying the Hawaiian words. I was on a mission.

I talked out loud to my tūtū and asked her for help. If anyone knew ʻōlelo, it was her, the mānaleo. She and I had been very close and even though she died when I was nine, I was lucky to have spent those short years getting to know her. I would call out to her and ask for her manaʻo. Sometimes, in the middle of translating sentences from English to Hawaiian, I would be thumbing through my trusty Hawaiian dictionary and even before I got to the word, I would hear the meaning whispered in my ear. It may seem kupaianaha* (wondrous), but that happened many times. For example, I would read a sentence in English out loud like, "That is a pleasant man." I would say, "Pleasant, pleasant, what is the Hawaiian word for pleasant?" Then I would go to my dictionary, and before I got to the meaning, in a small, quiet voice, I would hear, "'oluʻolu, ʻoluʻolu." When I turned to the page to look at the meaning, it would say, "'oluʻolu." That happened so many times I lost count. I never was afraid. My aunty says I'm special because of those kinds of Akua* kine tings.* (unexplainable and supernatural kinds of things).

During that time, I talked to co-workers, bosses, professors, and counselors and told them that I wanted to go back to school to

---

4   Hopkins, Ka Lei Haʻaheo Beginning Hawaiian Book

learn Hawaiian. I was wanting them to reassure me that I was doing the right thing to make a career change. I was already an insecure person, but that made me feel worse. In those days, there weren't many jobs that you could get with a Hawaiian language degree. They all told me the same thing. "What are you going to do with a degree in Hawaiian language? The only thing you can do is teach. You wanna be a teacher? The pay sucks. Why would you want to do that when you have a good job making good money? You have a business degree. Climb the corporate ladder. Hawaiian is a dead-end career." I am glad I did not listen to them.

It was one year later. I stuck it out in my "visa" job that I hated. After having a particularly bad day and getting into an argument at work with Amy, I called my parents. I complained about my job and then I told the truth. I told them everything that was going on. I said that I found my calling when I took the Hawaiian class. I loved it and wanted to go back to school to become a teacher. I said that I racked up thousands of dollars in credit card debt, and was paying way too much for my new car, apartment, and furniture. I told them I was stuck and asked if they could help. I remember breathing a sigh of relief when my dad said, "Go. We help you. We help you pay your bills and go back school. Go, go get your degree."

I shudder to think about what I would be doing today if my parents did not help me with my dream to get my teaching degree. That is why I had to make the wikiō with Kaipoʻi. That wikiō explains the mission of my life. I know that I must make sure that ʻōlelo Hawaiʻi lives on. In doing so, the Hawaiian mindset will also live on. As he said in the wikiō, "it is an indigenous way of looking at the world that can only be found here in Hawaiʻi."[5] This (Hawaiʻi) is the only place in the world where Hawaiian is spoken. There is too much at stake. So many of the customs, culture, and traditions of the past were lost. I must not and cannot let ʻōlelo Hawaiʻi

5   Ibid #2

die. As long as I live, teach, and share, it will live. E ola mau ka 'ōlelo Hawai'i.

Glossary of Chapter 6

1. E ola mau ka 'ōlelo Hawai'i – (EH-OH-LAH-MA-OO-KAH-OH-LEH-LOW-HAH-WAH-EEY) Hawaiian Proverb meaning, the Hawaiian Language lives on

2. Hawaiian Mindset[6] – thought or thinking process, way of looking at the world that can only be found in Hawai'i

3. Wikiō – (VEE-KEY-OH) video

4. Home language – the language most spoken in the home

5. 'Ōlelo No'eau – (OH-LEH-LOW-NO-EH-YOW) Hawaiian proverb

6. No'ono'o Hawai'i[7] – (NO-OH-NO-OH-HAH-WAH-EEY) the Hawaiian thought process, or as I call it, the Hawaiian mindset

7. Kupaianaha (KOO-PIE-AH-NAH-HAH) wondrous, strange

8. Akua – (AH-KOO-AH) unexplainable supernatural occurrences

9. Kine tings – Pidgin for kind of things

---

6   Ibid #2

7   Ibid #2

CHAPTER 7

MOE'UHANE; DREAM IN COLOR

The Parker Dictionary defines moe'uhane* as a dream; a vision; a trance.[1] Parker also did a makawalu* (deconstruct a Hawaiian Word into smaller words and define those words to get a comprehensive meaning) into moe* (to sleep) and 'uhane* (soul; spirit).

The book, "Nānā I ke Kumu Look to the Source," Volume 2 devotes chapter 4 to dreams and symbols. The following excerpts have been meaningful to me in understanding moe'uhane and allowing them to guide me:

Dreams and symbols[2]

In the old native culture, dreaming was a controlling and directing influence in the Hawaiian's life, particularly in fishing and planting, in house and boat building, in love and in war, in relation to birth and naming, to sickness and to death - E.S. Craghill Handy

Hōʻike na ka pō[3]

Dreams that reveal

---

1   Wehewehe Wikiwiki https://hilo.hawaii.edu/wehe/?q=moeuhane

2   Ukukau "Nana i ke kumu vol.2, p.169" http://www.ulukau.org/elib/cgi-bin/library?c=ql-cc2&l=en

3   Ukukau "Nana i ke kumu vol.2, pp.171-172 http://www.ulukau.org/elib/cgi-bin/library?c=qlcc2&l=en

Perhaps the dreams that most influenced Hawaiian waking hours were the ones classified as hōʻike na ka pō, "revelations of the night."

Hōʻike is literally "knowing, seeing, understanding." In the hōʻike of pō (night) what did one so know and understand?

One type of revelation was the glimpse into the future. This came in the moe piʻi pololei, or the clear, usually prophetic dream.

Moe piʻi pololei

The clear prophesy

"'Piʻi' means 'rise up.' 'Pololei' means 'straight,'" Mrs. Pukuʻi explains. "The moe piʻi pololei message came 'straight up.' It went 'straight to the point.' As soon as the dreamer woke up, he knew what his dream meant. This was often a prophesy. If the dream predicted death or injury of a quarrel or something terrible, then the only thing to do was to hoʻomānalo and ʻoki [remove] the harm or at least make it bearable."

However, not all prophetic dreams could be sweetened. Sometimes a frightening dream prophesy was recognized as inevitable. How? Co-author Pukuʻi gives the often-heard explanation for intuition.

"Sometimes you knew. You just knew."

A dream couched in symbol or riddle could, of course, be interpreted as prophesy. Or, the veiled prophetic dream might be recognized in retrospect. After some significant, perhaps tragic event, a previous dream might be remembered and interpreted as prediction and warning.

Cultural values live on in 1970s Hawaiian dreams[4]

Even when cultural symbols are absent from the dreams of present day Hawaiians, cultural values are very much present. There is a

---

4   Ukukau "Nana i ke kumu vol.2, p.188 http://www.ulukau.org/elib/cgi-bin/library?c=qlc-c2&l=en

prevailing tendency to dream of family concerns and relationships; a marked lack of dreams about work or career, employers, education, and examinations and achievement. There is communication between the dreamer and a deceased ancestor or senior member of the family line. All these dream characteristics are consistent with traditional values and beliefs of waking hours.

In two aspects of Hawaiian Dreaming we can form no conclusions:[5]

We do not know how the Hawaiian dream interpreter of tradition operates today. No wehewehe moe 'uhane (dream interpreter) would consent to an interview.

We cannot classify dream characteristics by the sex or by the age of the dreamer. The total of dreams studied was not large enough to do this.

However, we have a definite opinion on how Hawaiians put their dreams to use. Dr. McDermott expresses it:

"Hawaiians of the past had a system that was beautifully fitted to their culture. They were neither indifferent to their dreams nor terrified of them. They allowed their 'wandering spirit of sleep' to be a continuum of their daily lives. They made their dreams a creative and helpful force for the individual and for the group.

Many, but not all, Hawaiians of the present day continue to make this positive and beneficial use of dreams."

It was on the island of Kaua'i that I had my first significant dream about my life's purpose. It was a clear prophecy of the direction that

---

5   Ukukau "Nana i ke kumu vol.2, pp.205-206 http://www.ulukau.org/elib/cgi-bin/library?c=qlcc2&l=en

I was meant to go in. I was a haumāna* (student) starting 2nd-year papa ʻōlelo Hawaiʻi* (Hawaiian Language class). My kumu, Puhi, took our whole class on a week-long huakaʻi* (trip) to the neighbor island. We camped out in the Kapaʻa First Hawaiian Church's Community Hall and secluded ourselves away from other English speakers. The purpose of our trip was to ʻōlelo Hawaiʻi, no English speaking allowed.

I learned so much on that huakaʻi. I forced myself to ʻōlelo and carried my pocket Hawaiian dictionary with me everywhere I went. Our class went to the beach, the store, the gas station. Everywhere we went, we had to ʻōlelo. Everyday sayings like, "I gotta go eat, pee, wash my hands, take shower, etc." were things we said and heard all the time.

It was hard for me to express my thoughts and ideas without using Pelekānia* (English). Yet it was in that hard place that I grew the most. What would usually take me a few seconds to think of and say in Pelekānia, took me much longer to say in Hawaiian. Yet being forced to ʻōlelo became easier, and the thoughts and ideas rolled faster off of my alelo* (tongue). Sometime during that week, I gained the confidence to speak Hawaiian more flowingly.

On the last morning of our huakaʻi, I woke up after experiencing my first technicolor dream. My mouth felt dry and parched. I felt like I had been talking all night in Hawaiian. It was the first time I remember dreaming in color. In my dream, I was speaking fluently in Hawaiian. I was walking around talking to everyone. I talked non-stop about my feelings, my ideas, my goals, and my opinions. I was teaching people to ʻōlelo Hawaiʻi and telling them not to be afraid. I was encouraging them and told them to do everything they could to keep our ʻōlelo alive. I couldn't believe that I was so fluent. I was listening to others too and it was so easy to hoʻomaopopo* (comprehend). I could say and understand everything. In my dream, I was a kumu. I stood at a whiteboard teaching Hawaiian to kūpuna, mākua* (adults), ʻōpio* (teens), and keiki* (kids).

I was in a really deep sleep because I could hear my voice talking for a long time. I knew I was dreaming and moved into consciousness thinking about the sentence pattern that I was saying. I remember translating each word in my mind from Hawaiian to English. I said something in Hawaiian in a really loud voice and woke myself up. I sat up laughing because I remembered my dream so clearly. All the images in my head were so colorful and vivid. I couldn't stop smiling because I stopped talking mid-sentence, mid-Hawaiian sentence, not a mid-English sentence.

I was deeply moved in my naʻau. Like what Mrs. Pūkuʻi wrote in the dream chapter, I knew. I just knew. I knew that my ancestors, my kūpuna who had already passed on gave me that dream. I thought of my tūtū and I thanked her and all of them out loud. It was a clear picture of my future. I saw all the people that my life would impact. It was the clearest vision that I ever had up to that point in my life. It was the direction that I was meant to go in. It was them showing me that I must continue with ʻōlelo Hawaiʻi, and it was up to me to make sure that I continued in that direction.

It was a big kuleana. I could not grasp the huge magnitude of it at that time. I was in my 20s. I was just starting to live my grownup life. I felt an overwhelming feeling in my body, almost like a heavy weight on my shoulders. I was really glad, but I was scared too. I mostly felt unworthy. I felt that way because I was not a mānaleo. I tried to convince myself for a little while that maybe they gave me the wrong dream. But every time I tried to push it away, the bright colors in the dream of reds, greens, blues, yellows, whites, pinks, purples, and even colors that I couldn't describe, they reminded me of what I already knew. I knew like I knew. I knew.

Glossary of Chapter 7

1. Moeʻuhane – (MOY-OOH-HAH-NAY) dream
2. Makawalu[6] – (MA-KAH-VAH-LOO) Deconstructing and reconstructing literary constructives
3. Moe – (MOY) to sleep
4. ʻUhane – (OOH-HAH-NAY) soul; spirit
5. Haumāna – (HOW-MA-NAH) disciple, student, learner
6. Papa ʻōlelo Hawaiʻi – (PAH-PAH-OH-LEH-LOW-HA-WAH-EEY) Hawaiian Language - class
7. Huakaʻi – (WHO-AH-KAH-EEY) trip, journey
8. Pelekānia – (PAY-LAY-KAH-NEE-AH) English, British
9. Alelo – (AH-LEH-LOW) tongue, language
10. Hoʻomaopopo – (HO-OH-MA-OOH-POH-POH) to understand, to comprehend, from the word maopopo
11. Mākua – (MA-KOO-AH) parent, parents, adults
12. ʻŌpio – (OH-PEE-OH) youth, teenagers, teen
13. Keiki – (KAY-KEY) child, children

---

6   Definition from my notes at Papakū Makawalu Workshop (Edith Kanakaʻole Foundation January 2020)

CHAPTER 8

KU'U KUMU, MY TEACHER

The word kumu* means teacher, source, foundation, and the main stalk of a tree. I appreciate all kumu because of the waiwai* (wealth) of knowledge they impart to haumāna, the student. My 'ōlelo skills grew most when I began volunteering at a Hawaiian immersion preschool and worked with some of the kumu who were first language Hawaiian speakers from the island of Ni'ihau. That was over twenty years ago, so I can't remember all of their names.

One woman that I remember was Aunty Lolena. She is a mānaleo who is very prominent in the 'ōlelo Hawai'i community. On Ni'ihau, where she is from, Hawaiian is the main language spoken. The kids at the school call their female kumu 'anakē* (aunty) for respect, not misses, miss, or ma'am. We all called her 'Anakē Lolela.

The reason immersion schools are successful is because kids speak in Hawaiian, only in Hawaiian, every day, all day long. That is what immersion means. Immersion means that kids are "immersed" completely in the language. They learn all the subjects like math, science, reading, etc. through the target language, Hawaiian.

I experienced first hand how quickly kids (and myself) pick up the language when they are immersed in it. I saw 3-year-olds who were English only speakers come to the school for the first time. For several weeks, they didn't speak much, because they couldn't speak Hawaiian. But after hearing the ʻōlelo all the time five days a week, they got it. After about three to four weeks, they started speaking it. They picked it up very quickly. I have seen it happen time and time again.

One of the main ways that language is taught there is through songs. ʻAnakē taught a song that I never forgot. She taught it by singing it with the keiki in their daily circle time. It has so much meaning, and the kids loved singing with her. It's called "Kuʻu Kumu."[1] Here are the words and translation:

KUʻU KUMU	**MY TEACHER/TREE**
1. He lālā wau no kuʻu kumu	I am a branch of my teacher/tree
Nāna wau e koʻo mai	Who supports me
Inā ikaika ka makani	If the wind is strong
Nāna wau e aʻo mai	He teaches me
Luliluli, luliluli	Sway about, sway about
A laʻi mālie hou	Until all becomes calm again
2. He lālā wau no kuʻu kumu	I am a branch of my teacher/tree
Nāna wau e paipai mai	Who encourages me
Inā ikaika ka ua nui	If the rain is heavy
Nāna wau e aʻo mai	He teaches me
Uē ka lani, uē ka lani	The heavens weep, the heavens weep
A ola ka honua	And the earth lives

---

1   Pūnana Leo, Pai ka leo pp.6-7

3. He lālā wau no kuʻu kumu

I am a branch of my teacher/tree

Nāna wa u hoʻoulu mai

Who helps me to grow

Me nā lau wehiwehi

With lush, green leaves

Nāna wau e kuhi mai

He shows me

He pua ē, he pua ē

That I am a flower, a flower

Ke mōhala nei

That is beginning to bloom

In Hawaiian culture, kumu are everywhere. "Teachers" are not just found in the classroom. Hawaiian Akua whom we honor and respect are considered kumu. Some familiar Akua are Pele, Lono, Hina, Kamapuaʻa, Mauna a Wākea, Poliʻahu and Lilinoe. They teach us Hawaiian values through Hawaiian stories. They represent nature, places, plants, animals, etc. One such haʻawina* (lesson) comes from the story "The Breadfruit Tree."[2] It is about the Akua Kū*, whose kinolau* (physical manifestation) is the ʻulu* (breadfruit). The story goes:[3]

"Kū once came to Hawaiʻi and married a Hawaiian woman, with whom he lived many years and raised a large family. He did not tell the woman that he was a god; he worked on the land like anybody else.

A time came when food was scarce and no one could get enough to eat. Kū's wife and children were starving. Kū was sorry for them. He told his wife that he could get food for them by going on a long journey but that he could never return to them. At first, his wife would not hear of it, but she finally consented to his going when she heard the children crying with hunger. Kū said, "Let us go into the yard." There he said good-bye to the woman and told her that he was going to stand on his head and disappear into the

---

2   Pukuʻi/Green, He Mau Kaʻao Hawaiʻi "The Breadfruit Tree," pg.8

3   Ibid #2

earth. Then she must wait until his toes appeared out of the ground. Out of them would grow food for the family. He stood on his head and began to sink into the ground; first his head and shoulders, then finally his whole body disappeared.

His wife watched the spot every day and watered it with her tears. One day a sprout appeared, and from it a tree grew so rapidly that in a few days the family had the food that Kū had promised. It was the breadfruit. The wife and children ate all they wanted. Only they could pick the fruit; if anyone else tried, the tree would run back into the ground. After a time, sprouts grew about the parent tree, and these were given to friends and neighbors to plant in their own gardens. Thus Kū's gift blessed his people."

The kalo* (taro plant) teaches very important lessons. The extended family or 'ohana begins with the story of the kalo. Kalo is a generational plant. The word 'oha* (youngsters), derived from the word 'ohana, are the baby offshoots of the kalo plant. Kalo can be planted and grown over and over again. "The word "kalo," which is Hawaiian for taro, is used in two ways; It's the name for the entire plant, and more specifically it's the name for the plant's corm (the corm is the starchy section of underground stem that's used to make poi* - cooked, pounded, and watered down). To harvest the corm, each plant is uprooted, and the corm is separated from the green top or huli*. The huli is then carefully trimmed and replanted. Kalo farmers hold each individual plant in their hands, perform surgery on it and then grow it again, year after year. It's the most intimate form of agriculture imaginable."[4]

Kalo is not an "it" or a "thing" but rather a "he" in Hawaiian. The story of kalo's significance is that Wākea* (Sky Father) joined together with Papa* (Earth Mother). In their union a daughter, Ho'ohōkūkalani* (Making of the stars in the heavens) was born.

---

4   Hana Hou https://hanahou.com/14.2/kalo-man

Later, Wākea joined with Hoʻohōkūkalani and son #1 Hāloa* (Long quivering taro leaf stalk) was born as a stillbirth child. He was planted in the earth and later from that a kalo plant grew. Wākea and Hoʻohōkūkalani again mated and from that union came another son, Hāloa* #2 (long breath). He was born as a person, the first Hawaiian person. Since Hāloa #2 was the first kanaka, Hawaiian man, and his older brother Hāloa #1, was the kalo plant, kalo is elder to the Hawaiian people.

Nature provides many lessons. Hawaiians have an intimate relationship to nature. The value is explained in this ʻōlelo noʻeau, "He aliʻi ka ʻāina, he kauwā ke kanaka* (The land is chief, man is its servant)."[5]

I identify as a lifelong learner. I enjoy learning new things. That may be because I've had good kumu over the years. I've also had a few kumu who I didn't like, but I learned a lot from them too. Overall, I love the process of learning. That's part of the reason why I chose a career as a school teacher.

Kumu Puhi is a cherished kumu to me. He helped me by showing me how to apply my ʻōlelo skills in an everyday setting in the week-long huakaʻi. I went on three Hawaiian speaking huakaʻi with his classes. The first one I went on was as a student, and the other two were as his teacher's assistant. It was a blast because I got the experience of practicing being a teacher. It was also so much fun meeting new students and getting to practice my ʻōlelo skills with other new speakers. Puhi allowed me the opportunity to teach others. He started me on a journey to love Hawaiian language

5   Pukuʻi, ʻŌlelo Noʻeau 536

and grammar deeply. He also had a teaching style that made 'ōlelo interesting and was very fun for me. Mahalo nui iā 'oe, e Puhi.

I look to my kumu everywhere. My kūpuna are important kumu. One aspect of the Hawaiian mindset is to learn from my elders because they have experienced life. Younger people (not necessarily just younger in age, but younger in experience) look to older or more experienced people for guidance. I look to my kūpuna who are alive as well as to those who have passed on.

I give honor to the two women who had and continue to have, the most influence in shaping my life. They are my life's kumu, my mom, Pualani, and her sister, my Aunty Maile. Whenever I come to a hard place in my life, a joyous event, happy place, or come to a crossroads, I always consult with either of them. They are my special kūpuna.

Glossary of Chapter 8

1. Kumu – (KOO-MOO) besides teacher, kumu also means a tree
2. Waiwai – (VAH-EEY-WAH-EEY) wealth, valuables
3. 'Anakē – (AH-NAH-KAY) Aunty
4. Ha'awina – (HAH-AH-VEE-NAH) lesson
5. Kū – (KOO) Hawaiian deity representing war
6. Kinolau - (KEY-NOH-LAH-OOH) physical form of a Hawaiian deity
7. 'Ulu – (OOH-LOO) breadfruit, the physical plant form representing the Akua kū
8. Kalo – (KAH-LOH) taro or colocasia esculenta
9. 'Oha – (OH-HAH) offspring of kalo, baby corm

10. Poi – (POH-EEY) the Hawaiian staff of life, made from cooked taro corms, or rarely breadfruit, pounded and thinned with water[6]

11. Huli – (WHO-LEE) top of the taro that is replanted

12. Wākea – (WAH-KAY-AH) Sky Father, and the expanse of space

13. Papa also known as (Papahānaumoku) – (PAH-PAH) Earth mother, and all things that have a birth or regeneration cycle on earth[7]

14. Hoʻohōkūkalani – (HOE-OH-HOE-KOO-KAH-LAH-NEE) female child of Wākea and Papahānaumoku, making of the stars in the heavens

15. Hāloa #1 or Hāloanakalaukapalili – (HAH-LOW-AH-NAH-KAH-LA-OO-KAH-PAH-LEE-LEE) male child of Wākea and Hoʻohōkūkalani born as a stillbirth child, long quivering stalk of the taro leaf

16. Hāloa #2 – (HAH-LOW-AH) second male child of Wākea and Hoʻohōkūkalani who was believed to be the first Hawaiian man, long breath

17. He aliʻi ka ʻāina, he kauwā ke kanaka (HAY-AH-LEE-EEY-KAH-AYE-NAH-HAY-KAH-OO-WAH-KAY-KAH-NAH-KAH) – the land is chief, man is its servant, steward, caretaker

---

6   Wehewehe Wikiwiki https://hilo.hawaii.edu/wehe/?q=poi

7   Definition from my notes at Papakū Makawalu Workshop (Edith Kanakaʻole Foundation January 2020)

CHAPTER 9

HE HULIAU IA; A TIME OF CHANGE

He huliau ia* (It was a time of change). After Queen Liliʻuokalani* was overthrown in 1893, Hawaiʻi experienced great unrest. Her enemies, with the help of America, succeeded in taking over the Hawaiian Kingdom. Hawaiian nationalists and loyalists vowed to put her back in power. They staged a counter-revolution but were unsuccessful. Several years later, Liliʻuokalani officially protested. She documented her words in chapter 55 of her book:[1]

"I, Liliuokalani of Hawaii, by the will of God named heir apparent on the tenth day of April, A.D. 1877, and by the grace of God Queen of the Hawaiian Islands on the seventeenth day of January, A.D. 1893, do hereby protest against the ratification of a certain treaty, which, so I am informed, has been signed at Washington by Messrs. Hatch, Thurston, and Kinney, purporting to cede those Islands to the territory and dominion of the United States. I declare such a treaty to be an act of wrong toward the native and part-native people of Hawaii an invasion of the rights of the ruling chiefs, in violation of international rights both toward my people and toward friendly nations with whom they have made treaties, the

---

1   Liliuokalani, Hawaii's Story

perpetuation of the fraud whereby the constitutional government was overthrown and, finally, an act of gross injustice to me."

At the turn of the century in America, blacks and other people of color were dealing with institutional racism. Slavery was abolished in 1865, but Jim Crow laws were enacted to legalize and enforce racial segregation, prejudice, and hatred toward non-whites.

Lili'uokalani was not exempt from racism in the islands, even as queen. She was maligned, lied about, and treated with contempt. Political cartoons mocked her. Several cartoon caricatures show her pictured with Uncle Sam, the symbol of the USA. One portrayed her as a child being served food by him, another of her as a child sitting in a classroom at a desk being schooled by him, and another of her with a black face looking like a black Sambo female clown sitting on a seesaw controlled by him, the white savior.[2]

Yet, she was Hawaiian royalty, full of poise and grace in dealing with others until the very end. She yielded her throne to avoid bloodshed of her people. She further appealed to the President and Senate of the United States of America but was never reinstated even until death. She writes:[3]

"Therefore I, Liliuokalani of Hawaii, do hereby call upon the President of that nation, to whom alone I yielded my property and my authority, to withdraw said treaty (ceding said Islands) from further consideration. I ask the honorable Senate of the United States to decline to ratify said treaty, and I implore the people of this great and good nation, from whom my ancestors learned the Christian religion, to sustain their representatives in such acts of justice and equity as may be in accord with the principles of their fathers, and

---

2   Political Cartoons of the Kingdom of Hawai'i/Hawaiian Kingdom from various sites
     https://maoliworld.com/forum/topics/political-cartoons-of-the-kingdom-of-hawaii-hawaiian-kingdom-from?overrideMobileRedirect=1

3   Ibid #1

to the Almighty Ruler of the universe, to him who judgeth righteously, I commit my cause."

It took me two years to graduate with a professional diploma in secondary education in Hawaiian language. Because there was an extreme shortage of teachers in Hawai'i, UH offered a fast track program for people like myself with a degree in any subject to become a teacher. I got a degree with the intention of becoming a high school teacher. I planned to get my master's degree and then a doctorate in Hawaiian language. The end result would be to get a job as a UH instructor like Puhi. Somewhere after graduating, taking classes towards my master's, and becoming a teacher, I slowly veered off the path.

The biggest reason I went off track was that I made bad choices in men. My mom constantly told me to be careful in choosing friends. I followed her advice, but unfortunately, she never told me that was true of guys too. Nowadays, I am very aware of who I allow space and a place in my life.

Shortly after graduating, I took the first job that was offered to me as a Hawaiian immersion kindergarten teacher. I taught at an elementary school on the Wai'anae Coast. It was hard for me as a twenty-something-year-old new kumu. I was struggling in my personal life which affected my ability to teach. On the outside, I looked like I had my act together, but inside, I constantly doubted myself. There was so much drama with my boyfriend. We fought all the time and my distrust toward him did not help the situation. It drained me of my energy, zapped the life out of me, and made me almost quit on myself.

It didn't help that I was working with low-income students who had problems of their own. I saw first hand the devastating effects of poverty, homelessness, and drug abuse. It broke my heart that most of the people who lived there were natives. It was challenging to say the least, but they were some of the kindest kānaka* (Hawaiians) I had ever met. It was difficult for me as an empath. An empathic person feels other people's feelings which can lead to burnout if it's not managed and controlled. I would call a child's home whenever I sensed they were having problems, I would visit when they told me stories of their parents fighting, and I would bring food or supplies to their homes whenever I could. I was struggling.

On top of that, lessons in the Hawaiian language were limited. I spent hours and hours on the weekends developing and creating my own resources and translating curriculum from English to Hawaiian. I didn't like to ask for help or to get resources from other teachers. I didn't feel comfortable around the department head. I felt like she was micromanaging me, so I quit after two years.

My boyfriend and I were attending a non-denominational Christian church at the time. The pastor who counseled us said, "OK, God said you two are ready to get married." Foolishly, we did. With respect to my children, I won't go into any hurtful details of the marriage. I will say though that my relationship with him was doomed from the start. On the night we got back from Florida on our honeymoon (after arguing all week), I called my mom and told her I made a mistake. I felt like I was sinking in quicksand and had no way out. She told me that I had made my bed, and now I had to lie in it. She was from the old school "marriage for life" generation. I decided to follow through with the marriage vows that I took. Divorce would have caused me too much religious guilt anyway.

Three years later, I found myself pregnant. I was teaching at an intermediate school in Kāneʻohe and was not getting along with a few students and their parents. I felt unsupported by the principal and the administration like they weren't on my side to back me up. I had been teaching for five years in total. By that time the stress I was under at home and in school started to affect me. I wasn't happy teaching there. I thought about all my dreams and goals. I felt the burden to perpetuate my ʻōlelo and my dream to teach Hawaiian at the university. It seemed so far away. I had to quit.

My daughter, Hoʻoli, was coming soon, and we couldn't find anyone to watch her. Babysitters for newborns were running somewhere over $600 per month. We couldn't afford it, so one of us had to quit. I was the logical choice. Besides that, the stress was taking a toll on my mind and the pregnancy was taking a toll on my body. I had ballooned up to almost 230 pounds. I could barely walk because my feet were swollen. I felt sorry for my poor slippers!

It made sense for me to quit because I was a teacher. I was still torn up inside. I was always an independent woman, and now I was going to have to depend on my husband's money. On top of that, I felt like a quitter. I was bitter that I worked so hard to get my teaching degree and now had to quit my job to raise a kid.

On the last day of school, I cried. I cried, and cried, and cried. It was a bitter and hateful cry. I made angry growling sounds. I was mad at myself and mad at the world for the life that I had. It took me hours to pack up my belongings because I was tired from crying. I was sick and tired. I was packing up my life in those boxes, but I was also packing away all my hopes and dreams. I was supposed to teach ʻōlelo and change the world. Instead, I was going to become a stay at home mom to change shitty diapers.

Glossary of Chapter 9

1. Huliau – (WHO-LEE-OW) Turning Point, time of change[4]

2. Liliʻuokalani – (LEE-LEE-OOH-OW-KAH-LAH-NEE) the last reigning Queen of Hawaiʻi overthrown in 1893.

3. Kānaka – (KAH-NAH-KAH) Hawaiians [plural]/kanaka [singular] (see Chapter 17 for other definition)

---

4   Wehewehe wikiwiki https://hilo.hawaii.edu/wehe/?q=huliau

CHAPTER 10

HOʻONANI I KA MAKUA MAU; RELIGIOUS DOGMA

When the New England Missionaries came to Hawaiʻi, they brought their religious faith and dogma. The Webster Dictionary defines dogma as "something held as an established opinion; a point of view or tenet put forth as authoritative without adequate grounds; a doctrine or body of doctrines concerning faith or morals formally stated and authoritatively proclaimed by a church."[1]

They also brought music that drew Hawaiians in droves. These songs called religious hymns were noted in the missionaries writings:[2]

"Mission journals note how pleased the Hawaiian people seemed with the new music and how they came by the hundreds to hear the hymns. The rising and descending scales were completely different from the Hawaiians' traditional system of tones and pitches, and initially caused difficulty. The resourceful Reverend Hiram Bingham established an evening singing school, where his eager pupils not only practiced Western musical scales, but also learned the Bible by chanting its verses in their traditional mele rhythms. It was the birth of modern Hawaiian music, a harmony

---

1   Merriam-Webster Dictionary https://www.merriam-webster.com/dictionary/dogma

2   Ariyoshi, Hawaii: National Geographic Traveler 4th edition, p. 41

of New England hymns infused with the beautiful poetic form and ancient rhythms of Hawaii.

The singing schools spread throughout the islands and Hawaiians were quickly composing their own songs in the new genre. The first hymnal, Na Himeni Hawaii: He Me Ori ia Iehova, Ke Akua Mau (Hawaiian Hymns and Songs to Jehovah, the Eternal God), was published in 1823 and contained 47 songs, including the classic, "Iesu Me Ke Kanaka Waiwai (Jesus and the rich man)."

Some of the hymns they sang in English were translated into ʻōlelo Hawaiʻi. They did this so that Hawaiians could understand their faith, sing their hymns, and convert to believing in their god. The song "Praise God from Whom all Blessings Flow"[3] was one of those songs. It was written by Reverend Hiram Bingham. The "Doxology" or "Hoʻonani" as we call it today, is the Hawaiian version of that song. I sang this song in church every Sunday from the time I was born until the time I moved away for college. I know the words by heart:

Hoʻonani i ka Makua mau

Ke Keiki me ka ʻUhane nō

Ke Akua mau, hoʻomaikaʻi pū

Ko kēia ao, ko kēlā ao

ʻĀmene

Praise God from whom all blessings flow

Praise Him all creatures here below

Praise Him above, ye heavenly hosts

Praise Father, Son, and Holy Ghost

Amen

---

3   Hoʻonani or Doxology https://www.huapala.org/ChristReligious/Hoonani_Ka_Makua.html

I settled into my life as a wife and mother. The marriage was rocky and I needed something to fill the void that 'ōlelo Hawai'i left. I turned to God and the church. It was the music of the church that drew me in.

Music made me feel comfortable because that's what we did at our family get-togethers since I was a kid. Some weekends and on most holidays, in the early evening, my 'ohana gathered together. Everybody always brought something, potluck style. Locals* consider it rude to come to a party empty-handed. The real magic started when someone would break out their 'ukulele, guitar, or other homemade instruments like the spoons or the pakini* bass (a washtub or tin pail turned upside down) if we were lucky. We sang all night until the last person left. Those smoky backyard barbecues were called pā'ina* (parties). I can still smell the Kool Milds, Budweiser beer, and barbecue meat from the grill. A party where people get together and make music is called a kanikapila* (jam session). The interaction of food, fellowship, and music has always been a way of life in the islands.

The church became my life. It was a new age Charismatic Christian non-denominational church with thousands of members. The vibe was young, hip, and forward-thinking. It was cool, and I was cool because I was a part of it.

I joined the choir with about fifty other singers. We sang at services on Sunday at 7 a.m., 9 a.m., 11 a.m., and 6 p.m., and a Wednesday midweek service at 7 p.m. Church was all day on Sundays and other meetings during the week included Wednesday night service, bible study group, leadership meetings, and choir rehearsals.

I got promoted to be a lead singer about two years after I started attending the church. It required a bigger commitment. I barely saw my family and the time away from them contributed to the already existing problems in the marriage. I was so busy that I hardly had time for anything else. If I wasn't working, I was at church. I loved singing but I had forgotten my commitment to perpetuate the 'ōlelo. When my daughter was just four years old, my kūpuna watching over me reminded me of it.

I took a job at my church's school. The church had a pre-k-12 school, and I got hired there. I was still hesitant about going back to teaching full-time so I took a part-time job as a teacher's assistant. I noticed that the Hawaiian immersion preschool was on the same street as my church. My husband and I agreed to enroll my daughter Ho'oli there. I barely spoke Hawaiian at all anymore, so I thought it was great.

I dropped her off every morning, then walked down the street to my job and would pick her up in the afternoons after pau hana* (finished work). My heart swelled up with pride every morning when I dropped her off as I heard 'ōlelo Hawai'i coming from everywhere, the kumu, the haumāna, and the 'ohana.

The preschool at my job was reasonably priced. Since I was an employee, the tuition cost would be cut in half if my daughter attended our school. It did not matter to me. I was happy paying double the cost of our school's tuition because Ho'oli was learning the 'ōlelo. Some fellow staff members at work asked me why my daughter was not attending our school. It made sense to enroll her in our school since I worked there. I always politely said to them, I can teach her about God at home. I want her to perpetuate the Hawaiian language because we are Hawaiians. One day as I was walking past my boss's office, her secretary popped out and signaled me inside. She asked if she could speak to me privately. My boss wasn't there so I wondered why she wanted to talk to me. I agreed and sat down on the other side of her desk looking at the frown on her face. I thought I was in trouble for something I had done.

She was a leader in the church, an older Hawaiian wahine* (woman), someone I looked up to and considered a mentor. She was very close to my boss as they both attended the church and worked together for a long time. She asked me why Hoʻoli was attending the Hawaiian preschool. I gave her the usual answer of, "Well, I can teach her about God at home anytime. We are Hawaiians and we need to perpetuate our language." Up until that point, everyone agreed with me. But not her, she said, "Well I am Hawaiian too, but we are Christians first. She should not be attending that school, she should be here at ours learning about God and his word. God is more important than Hawaiian". Her religious dogma shook me up for a little while. I didn't have an answer for her but I wondered if she was right.

I went home and I prayed. Instead of listening to her words, I lifted my prayers and asked the Lord for guidance. I was reminded of the story in the bible when God introduced Himself to Moses at the burning bush. In Exodus, Chapter 3, Moses saw a bush on fire. The flames burned bright but the bush never got consumed or burned up. When Moses got closer, God said to him[4], "I am the God of <u>your ancestors</u>, the God of Abraham, the God of Isaac, and the God of Jacob." Then God said, [5] "I have certainly seen the affliction of <u>my people</u> who are in Egypt, and I have heard their cry…"

---

4   International Standard Version Bible, Book of Exodus Chapter 3, verse 6

5   International Standard Version Bible, Book of Exodus Chapter 3, verse 7

There was my answer, her dogma was wrong. God cares about race. He is the God of Moses' ancestors and the God of Moses' people, the Hebrews (Israelites). If he didn't care about them then he would not have said so. I believe that God cares about me, my people, and my race. My people are Hawaiian.

Glossary of Chapter 10

1. Locals – the term for people who are born and raised in Hawai'i or have been living in the islands for a long time

2. Pakini - (PAH-KEY-NEE) homemade washtub bass instrument

3. Pā'ina – (PAH-EEY-NAH) party

4. Kanikapila – (KAH-NEE-KAH-PEE-LAH) small kine music jam session, literally means to sound the instrument

5. Pau hana – (POW-HAH-NAH) finished working

6. Wahine/wāhine – (WAH-HEE-NAY) woman, female [singular]/ women, females [plural]

CHAPTER

11 HAKUMELE; WRITE MUSIC

Hakumele* means to compose or write music, songs, chants, etc, and also means a person who composes those things. The meaning becomes clearer in the makawalu. Haku means to compose and mele, as we learned previously, is a song or a chant. Hawaiian songwriting is very different from English songwriting. Mele Hawai'i* (Hawaiian Songs/Music) typically reflect the ideas and values of this place just as other songs of cultures elsewhere reflect their own special place in the world.

I took a Hawaiian hakumele class at UH from Kumu Puakea when I was studying to become a teacher. Many of the lessons made me look deeper into mele and their lyrics, melodies, and meanings. It was interesting to discover the word choices used by the hakumele and the placement of those words.

Hawaiians had a deep connection to the earth. They had over 200 words for ua* (rain), as compared to English (rain, storm, drizzle, sprinkle, etc.). In the Hawaiian language, there were many words describing the sea, ocean, rain, trees, plants, etc. "The most comprehensive record of its kind that compiles this extensive part of Hawaiian's vocabulary, sourcing its oral tradition, mele (song), oli (chants), mo'olelo (stories), 'ōlelo no'eau (proverbs) and written literature."[1] In the book, "Hānau ka Ua, Hawaiian Rain Names," author, Collette Leimomi Akana writes about the Hawaiian words for rain. She says, "To our kūpuna, the winds and rains were more than just elements. They had a familial connection to them. There are so many chants and songs that talk about these winds and rains by name, and the connection our kūpuna had with them."[2] "Our kūpuna were so attuned to their environment that they assigned individual names to the multitude of winds and rains occurring throughout the archipelago... I believe they named each wind and rain because they encountered them almost daily and felt a kinship with them."[3]

Songwriting styles slowly change over time. One thing that remains in mele, is the use of kaona* (deeper meaning). Kaona is expressed through the song "Kona Kai 'Ōpua. This song proudly speaks of Kona, my beloved home on the Moku o Keawe* (Hawai'i Island). The hakumele is Henry Waiau who wrote this in 1941.[4] The song uses love for place and kaona in the meaning below:[5]

Ha'aheo Hawai'i na Kona	Proud is Kona of Hawai'i
Ka wai kau i ka maka ka 'ōpua	The waters and thick clouds
Hualalai kau mai i luna	Hualalai, the majestic mountain
E ka makani ahe olu wai	With the refreshing wind
'O ka pa konane ahe kehau	The bright moonlight that
I ka ili o ka malihini	Beckons the visitors

1   Hawai'i Magazine https://www.hawaiimagazine.com/content/hawaiians-have-more-200-words-rain

2   Hawai'i Public Radio https://www.hawaiipublicradio.org/post/rain-born-hanau-ka-ua#stream/0

3   Ibid #1

4   Mondoy Music http://www.mondoymusic.com/MM_Choir/chr_ahahimeni_composers.htm

5   Huapala.org https://www.huapala.org/Ko/Kona_Kai_Opua.html

Hui:	Chorus:
Hanohano	Proud
'O Kona kai 'ōpua i ka la'i	The cloud banks over Kona's peaceful sea
'O pua hinano i ka mālie	Like the hinano flower
Wai na lai	In the peaceful sea
Ka mako a 'ōpua	The cloudbanks of Kona
'A'ole no ahe lua a'e like aku ia	Are incomparable, second to none
Me Kona kai 'ōpua	The cloudbanks of Kona
Ke kai ma'oki'oki	The streaked sea
Ke kai malino a'o Kona	The peaceful sea of Kona
Kona kai 'ōpua i ka la'i	The cloud bank over Kona's peaceful sea
'O pua hinano i ka mālie	Like the hinano flower in the calm
Holo na wai a ke kehau	Where dusk descends with evening dew
Ke na'u wai la nā kamali'i	The na'u is chanted by the playful children
Kāohi ana i ke kukuna lā	Hold back the rays of the sun
Ku'u la kolili i ka 'ili kai	The sun rays reflecting on the surface of the sea
Pumehana wale ho'i ia 'āina	Very warm is the land

Aloha no kini aʻo Hoʻolulu	Very loving the Hoʻoulu progeny
ʻAʻohe lua ia ʻoe ke aloha	Nothing compares to the love
O kuʻu puni o ka mea ʻowa	O my beloved companion of all time
Haʻina ka inoa o kuʻu lani	For my lovely chief, my last refrain
No Liholiho no ka inoa	Liholiho, I praise your name
Kahea: He Inoa No Liholiho	Call: The Name of Liholiho

"Source: Stanich Collection - This mele tells of a love affair between Liholiho (Kamehameha II) and a woman of rank. It sings of the places and activities of Kona and compares them to the deep emotions of love. Known as Kona of the tranquil seas, the ʻōpua or pink cumulus cloud formations that hang low, are regarded as omens of good fortune and good weather. Hinano is the blossom of the male pandanus tree and was used as an aphrodisiac. Naʻu is a game of Kona where the children chant "naʻu" and hold their breath until the sun disappears. Hoʻolulu was an ancient chief of Kona…"

On the first day of hakumele class, I almost dropped out. Kumu Puakea handed out the syllabus, then announced that all of us would haku our own mele. We had the whole semester to work on it but that would be our final project. The last day of class would be our hōʻike* (test) where we would be performing the mele that each

82

of us wrote. My mind was saying, "What did he say? Did he say I had to write a song? Sing it for my classmates? On the last day of school? By myself? Wait, I had to haku my own mele in Hawaiian? Did he know that I never wrote a song in any language before?" Auē* (oh goodness)!

Fast forward to 2012, and I was still singing. I had been promoted to lead singer of my church's new Kona branch. It was a chance to see my family on the weekends since most of my ʻohana still lived there. I had been living on Oʻahu for over 20 years by that time and would usually only see my dad, mom, and sister about once a year. This would give me the ability to fly home on Saturday night, practice with my Kona choir team, sleepover at my parents' house that night, sing at Sunday morning church service, then drag myself back to the airport, hop a plane, and go back home to Oʻahu. It was a great experience for me but my life was unraveling.

I heard a voice in my ear. I cannot remember if it was an audible voice or a voice in my head, but it was definitely a voice. It sounded like rustling and whispering in my ear. My first recollection of it was in early 2014. It echoed over and over. The whispers went on for months with me hearing but taking no action. It wasn't a scary voice or a nagging voice. It was gentle and constant, a library voice.

A "library voice" is the voice used while in the library, of course. I used that voice mostly during the summertime. My preteen summer days were spent with my cousin Iwa (two syllables like Eeyore but pronounced EEY-VAH). We hung out and played together a lot. She was deaf, but she could read lips and she taught me American Sign Language (ASL). Some days Iwa and I would walk or get dropped off at the Kealakekua Library. I got super excited because we stayed all day usually, till Iwa's mom, Aunty Koko, picked us up to go home. Iwa would read anime and draw all kinds of stuff, mostly cartoon characters with big faces and huge eyes. I read mystery books, like Nancy Drew but liked to giggle and "library voice" with my cousin. I like library voices.

All of my kūpuna were speaking sweetly and collectively together to me. I enjoyed hearing them. "Write music, write music," they said. "I can do it," I answered out loud. "I did it before in haku-mele class, and I can do it again." Granted, it was a long time ago, like 20 years. But a whole album? It felt like they were saying that I was supposed to write a whole album. I felt an urgency to do it. The urgency was kinda like the feeling you have when you gotta go mimi* (pee) or ki'o* (poop). You can hold off, but the feeling stays until you go to the bathroom. If you wait too long, the conse-quences are not good. But once you do it, it's a relief.

My life was too busy and something needed to give. I knew I couldn't write meaningful songs while being involved in so many things. I had never experienced "the voice" so loud and so often. It was something that had never happened before, not like that. God, the Holy Spirit, Jesus, my kūpuna, all voices telling me to write music and it was getting louder. They were still whispering, but on a scale of 0-10, with 0 being silence and 10 being a yell or scream, it was a 3-4. The old whisper was between a 1-2.

I was living a lie. It looked like my life was great on the out-side but looks can be deceiving. I was wearing a mask. The mask I wore was of a happy lady, always smiling and laughing, having it all together. That couldn't be further from the truth. I was running 'em haahd* (going all out). I was working full-time at a hotel in Kapolei, Monday through Friday, five days a week. I barely saw my children because I worked weekdays and was off-island on the weekends. I felt guilty about not spending time with them, but I didn't want to be at home because of the strained marriage. I did whatever I could to stay gone.

I was stressed out and started getting bad headaches in the morning after I woke up. I had occasional headaches in the past, but I noticed that I woke up with headaches more often. My teeth and jaw were sore in the morning. I used a mouth guard that my dentist prescribed for teeth grinding. I had always been a teeth grinder, even when I was a kid. I'm the type of person that holds stress inside without telling others or letting it out. My dentist was concerned. I was concerned because the headaches were getting worse. My mouth guard was so grounded down that I had to buy a new one. If you have ever seen a mouth guard, like the ones prescribed by a dentist, they are durable, similar to the ones boxers use. I told my dentist about it and he warned me to take care of myself. He told me that grinding adds hundreds of pounds of stress on the teeth and told me that the migraines were the result of grinding. My body was trying to tell me that I was not handling my life well. I needed to change.

I quit everything. I went from one extreme, extremely busy, to another extreme, extremely free. I quit every activity, everything except for my job. It was a shock. My family had to adjust too. They were not used to seeing me all the time. In the past, I blew in and out of their lives. I was traveling for three years, and now I was home. At first, I didn't know what to do with myself. I was tired from years of being busy. I had lost my passion for the ʻōlelo so again my kūpuna had to remind me.

"Write music, write music," they said. I started to write. It was a healing session. As I wrote, I realized that I had been stuffing a lot of things, bad things, way down deep inside. It was like the mimi/kiʻo analogy. It all came gushing out. Hurts, pains, disappointments, misery, heartbreak, fear, and love. You name it, I felt it. I had stuffed it all down inside me and now it was bubbling up and shooting out. I wrote songs and tried to express feelings so the listener could feel my emotions with me. I was seriously considering divorce and had to face it. I was feeling very sad. It took about two months for me to finish 11 songs.

- In 2015, I finished the album. I wrote and recorded 11 songs. The songs ranged in mana'o* (meaning):

- Song 1: Ka 'Uhane Hemolele (Kahiau) -the title track, slow religious song giving honor to my Heavenly Father, with kaona honoring my dad, mom, and two children Ho'oli, and Hi'ilani

- Song 2: Ola Mau – Fast percussion song honoring kūpuna which included a new bridge section chanted by my mom, the first song I ever wrote in hakumele class

- Song 3: Lei Mekia – a religious song about the messiah

- Song 4: What Would I Do? – a fun upbeat song for my two daughters

- Song 5: The other side – a slow contemporary ballad about people struggling with mental illness and suicide, written for my friend Lore after she told me about her struggle in this area

- Song 6: He mele nō iā Kāne'ohe – fast tempo song honoring the windward side of O'ahu with kaona honoring my sister Barbie

- Song 7: Marah – a fictional ballad about a woman named Marah who had a difficult relationship with her mother, written after a friend had talked to me about her life with an absent father

- Song 8: Pick up the pieces – upbeat contemporary song encouraging myself and others to move on after a failed relationship

- Song 9: Hauʻoli Lā Hānau Prelude - introduction to song 10
- Song 10: Hauʻoli Lā Hānau – a capella happy birthday song sung with my daughters
- Song 11: Ka ʻUhane Hemolele (Kahiau) Instrumental - ʻukulele instrumental version of Ka ʻUhane Hemolele (Kahiau) song 1 performed by my friend Corey Fujimoto who played most of the ʻukulele on my album

Glossary of Chapter 11

1. Haku – (HAH-KOO) to compose as in a song, or to braid as in a lei
2. Hakumele – (HAH-KOO-MEH-LAY) Songwriting or songwriter
3. Mele Hawaiʻi (MEH-LEH-HAH-VAH-EEY) Hawaiian music or songs
4. Kaona – (KAW-OO-NAH) deeper or hidden meaning
5. Moku o Keawe – (MOH-KOO-OH-KAY-AH-VAY) Hawaiʻi Island, Big Island of Hawaiʻi
6. Hōʻike – (HOE-EEH-KAY) test, show, exhibit
7. Auē – (OW-EY) (interjection) Oh goodness!
8. Mimi – (MEE-MEE) to urinate, to go pee
9. Kiʻo – (KEY-OH) to defecate, to go poop
10. Run ʻem haahd – Pidgin for going all out, go all the way
11. Manaʻo – (MA-NAH-OH) meaning, intention (see Chapter 5 for other definition)

CHAPTER 12

OLA MAU; MOVING ON

Ola mau* means to live on forever. Ola means life, and mau means to continue, perpetuate, for eternity. "Ola Mau" is the name of the song that I wrote in my hakumele class. I wrote it on the premise that our kūpuna are the backbone of our existence. We live on because of our elders. We live on through the knowledge and information that they passed down to us. We follow our valuable kūpuna as explained in the song lyrics below:[1]

Pauku 1:	Verse 1:
Ola mau, ola mau	Live on, perpetuated
Hulu manu, hulu manu ē	Royalty, bird feathers (symbol of our elders whom we value)
Hui:	Chorus:
E Nānā mai i ka beauty	Look at the beauty
I ka nani o Hawai'i	Beauty of Hawai'i
He waiwai nui nā kūpuna	Elders who are valued
Hulu kupuna o kākou	Our prized elders

---

1   Tracie Keolalani on Apple Music: https://music.apple.com/us/album/ola-mau/1027472000

Pauku 2:	Verse 2:
Ola mau, ola mau	Live on, perpetuated
Waele mua i ke ala ē	(Our elders) who clear the path for us to travel
Oli:	Chant:
He mēheuheu mai nā kupuna ē	The elders made that path that we follow
I paʻa i nā kupuna ʻaʻole kākou e puka	If it weren't for our elders we wouldn't have come forth
E mālama iā lākou nei	Care for them
Ola nā iwi	The bones live on
Ola nā kūpuna	The elders
He hulu aliʻi	Their royal legacy (Royal bird feathers were used to make cloaks
He hulu manu	for chiefs. The feathers symbolize the chiefly status)
He hulu kūpuna ē	Our prized elders
Pauku 3:	Verse 3:
Ola mau, ola mau	Live on, perpetuated
Mēheuheu mai nā kupuna ē	The way handed down from our elders
Pauku 4:	Verse 4:
Ola mau, ola mau	Live on, perpetuated

Ola mau nā iwi ola ē

The bones live (respected elder well cared for by family)

My kūpuna were telling me to write music because it brought healing to my life. I trusted that they were guiding me in the direction that was best for me. I know that they will always guide me in the direction that is best and in the direction toward fulfilling my destiny.

To live on, ola mau, I knew that I had to move on. It was time, seventeen years was a long time. I had been afraid of moving on. There would be the stigma of being known as a "divorcee" once I made up my mind to do it. I rationalized that it would be better for my kids if I stayed married, but that was an excuse. I was afraid of being alone and I was afraid that people would reject me once I was divorced. I remember the scripture,[1] "God hates divorce." There would be consequences once I made that decision. I made up my mind to do it anyway. "God hates divorce," yes, but as long as it didn't say, "God hates me," then I'd be okay with the consequences.

Stigmas, rules, and social norms can cause serious head trips and emotional damage. Growing up, I heard things like "pull yourself together," "control yourself," "you're not thinking straight," "get a grip," "don't be weak," "get your shit together." Mental health issues were seen as weaknesses and not as strengths. They weren't seen as injuries that needed fixing. Broken heads and broken hearts need treatment just the same as broken arms and

---

1   International Standard Version Bible, Book of Malachi Chapter 2, verse 16

broken legs do. Humans were not meant to press through emotional issues. We were meant to deal with and work through issues, not ignore or run away from them.

It may be a machismo thing or an American thing to sweep emotions under the rug and not show feelings. I have a friend from South America who said that most people in her country see a psychologist regularly. They take their emotional well-being seriously. I was emotionally drained and didn't want to end up in another relationship like the last one that I had been in. I had never gone to a therapist or psychologist in the past. I thought they were for crazy people or mentally unstable people but I was desperate and needed help. I knew that if I didn't change, my natural tendencies, insecurities, and energetic frequencies would lead me to a relationship like the one I'd just gotten out of. I'm not blaming my ex-husband at all. I am 100% responsible for every decision I made in the past and every decision I will make in the future, good and bad. I needed counseling.

I needed help, professional help. I was broken. I don't know if my head was broken but some things in my head needed healing, that's for sure. I don't believe anybody leaves a long-term marriage or relationship and doesn't need a few things in their head fixed. It took a few tries until I found Dr. Wang. She was the right fit and I felt at ease the first time I met her. I was surprised that talking to her helped me so much. We got along really well, and she gave me no-nonsense advice with no sugarcoating it. She gave me homework assignments and exercises to practice. She helped me see my life's situations from another perspective, a healthier perspective. She was a straight-talker no bullshit just straight to the point. I must have cried the whole time in my sessions for the first two months straight.

Slowly but surely, my life has changed for the better. I've been seeing her for several years now, and I do a once a month check-in with her. I continue to do the hard work outside of sessions. I read books, write in my daily journal, watch Ted Talks, and listen to podcasts by people who I admire like Oprah Winfrey and Brene Brown. I've experienced so much healing. My life is peaceful, tranquil, and calm. I am the happiest I have ever been in my entire life. I feel healthy inside and out.

My children needed counseling too after the divorce. They got a divorce just as I did. They had to make the move from one parent's home to two parents' homes. They had to adjust their schedules. They spent one week at their dad's house then packed everything up and moved to my house. After that week, they packed up again and went back to their dad's. The next week, back to my house. The cycle never stopped.

I juggled counseling sessions every other week for all of us along with school, sports, and homework for the girls. I took them to a therapist that specialized in children's therapy. I wanted to make sure that they were ok and had an adult to talk to besides their dad or me.

After six months Hoʻoli said she didn't need the counseling sessions anymore. "What? No, no, you can't stop going to therapy, you need to express your feelings and emotions," I said. She told me, "I don't need therapy anymore. I am fine." "It's only been a few months, you need more sessions," I said. "Mom, I'm good. I am happy that you're divorced. You are happier now. We are happy that you are happy. We like it this way," she said.

A month later Hiʻilani said, "Mom if Hoʻoli can quit, can I quit too?" "No, you need to keep going because you need to talk about your feelings," I said. "We just draw pictures and play," she said. "Well, I want you to talk to her about any feelings you have about the divorce and how you are adjusting to going back and forth between dad and me," I told her. "She's weird. I don't like her. I don't need a kid's therapist. We draw pictures and play and I'm too old for that. I'll talk to myself when I need therapy," she said. I laughed, "You crack me up. Ok, you can quit."

I learned something from my girls. Intrinsically, kids know and understand the dynamics of marriage. They may or may not be able to express it in words, but they are smart enough to know what is going on. They want to be happy but they won't be happy when they see fighting and arguing all the time. Acting doesn't work either. My kids knew that even when I tried to fake being happy on the outside, I was miserable on the inside. I will never forget Ho'oli's words, "when you're happy, we're happy." We're moving on.

Glossary of Chapter 12

1. Ola – (OH-LAW) life
2. Mau – (MAW-OO) forever, to continue
3. Ola mau – (OH-LAH-MAW-OO) to live on, immortal

CHAPTER 13

HOLOHOLO; WE GO CRUISE

The word holoholo* (to go fishing, gathering flowers, or other types of activity) has several meanings. I understand it to be something of a code word with a hidden meaning. It means to go fishing or pick flowers up ma uka* (up in the mountains), or do some type of activity, without revealing the actual activity itself.

Growing up, Aunty Maile told stories about how Grandma Frances would load up all the kids in the car and take them to the beach. She planned to catch fish and other seafood for their meal, but whenever they asked where she was taking them, she said, "We going holoholo." They knew what that meant. Aunty said that Hawaiians believe that fish can hear what you say. If you say that you are going to go "catch fish" they will hear you and then will run away. The result is that you will have no catch, or a poor catch after speaking those words. That's the reason why whenever grandma took them to the beach, she would say that they were going "holoholo." She knew what she was planning to do and where she was planning to go. She knew her destination and purpose, but her intention was always veiled.

My mom said that they spoke this way because they were in tune with their environment. They were connected to their surroundings, so much so that even words uttered far away from the beach (the nearest beach was about two miles from their home) would be heard by living creatures over there. An ʻōlelo noʻeau that brings understanding is, "Aia nō i ke au a ka wāwae,"[1] which translates, "whichever current the feet go in. Hawaiians did not like to be asked where they were going and this was the usual answer given when so asked. It was felt that discussing any business such as fishing or birdcatching beforehand results in failure."[2]

Even though this type of thinking was normal to my mom and her ʻohana, it may be thought of as "strange" or "superstitious" to outsiders. The first analogy to bring a clearer understanding to someone who may not understand them is in the bible verse, "Words can bring death or life! Talk too much, and you will eat everything you say."[3] Too many times, people say things they don't mean whether good, bad, or indifferent. "Let's get together sometime. Call me. Let's do lunch," they say. They speak empty words, words that hold no weight or value. The second is, "The Walls have ears,"[4] which means that someone may be listening. Take heed and be careful of what you say.

The other meaning of holoholo* (going out for pleasure, riding) was what we called cruising* (or hanging out) with no set plans except having a good time. I would call my friends on the phone in high school and say, "What you doing? We go cruise."

---

1 Pukuʻi, ʻŌlelo Noʻeau 68

2 Ibid #2

3 Contemporary English Version Bible, Book of Proverbs Chapter 18, verse 21

4 Quote credited to Dionysius, the Greek tyrant of Syracuse

Holoholo is great when you have time to kill. It was good when I was younger because I went with the flow and did what everyone else was doing. I didn't think about what I was going to do with my life. I often heard the question, "What do you want to do when you grow up?" Even when I was in college, my major was liberal arts for several years. Majoring in liberal arts meant I couldn't decide on a real major. My mom was the one who suggested I go into business. And so, like a good girl who wants to please people, I got my degree in international business.

I never forgot my moeʻuhane in color. Years later it was still magnificent. I believed it was my kūpuna who laid out my purpose in front of me. I was lucky to find it in my early twenties. Some people went their whole lives never knowing what they were put here on earth to do. I KNEW I was supposed to preserve my ʻōlelo Hawaiʻi. It was my passion. The problem was that I was naïve.

They hoodwinked me, the movie and TV shows that is. I watched too many dumb shows that were dangerous to my thinking. The shows I grew up with deceived me into believing that I needed a man. The underlying storyline said that I needed a man to take care of me and to make me happy. Cinderella was my favorite Disney fairytale. I fantasized about the day that my Cinderella fantasy would become a reality. I wanted to be Cinderella. I wanted to live happily ever after. I wanted the rich white prince in the white tuxedo to drop into my life and make everything alright. I was only half a person without him. He would complete me. His purpose in life would become my purpose in life. I was waiting to ride off into the sunset into our happily ever after. The problem was, Prince Charming was a fairytale and he was never going to come.

By the time I was divorced in 2016, I was frustrated. I was frustrated that my life had not turned out the way that I imagined it or pictured it to be. I was a middle-aged divorcee with two kids stuck in a dead-end job that I was hating more and more each day. My job entailed babysitting kids at a hotel, for god's sake. I was so far away from my dream of perpetuating my ʻōlelo. I was frustrated that I had waited so long to get divorced. Seventeen years was a long time. I was stuck in the holoholo phase.

Why was I so far away from my purpose in life? I was relatively young and in good health, but would men be interested in a forty something-year-old lady with two kids? Dating twenty years ago was totally different. There was no internet, cell phones, or dating apps back then. I was unsure of how to navigate my way now because it felt foreign to me. Long ago, I would meet a guy in person, and instantly know if I wanted to get to know him and if we had chemistry or not. That's how I met my ex-husband, in person, at a club.

Online dating seemed so strange and sterile. Looking on my phone at some random dude's picture on a dating app and reading his bio didn't interest me. I remember watching the documentary, "Catfish," a few years back and wondering how I would be able to tell whether a guy was real or not. My friend told me that a guy could be a "bot." "Online dating is how people meet nowadays," she said. I had questions, "What if I get rejected? What if he thinks I'm too old? What if my friends see my online profile or worse, my students? What will they think?" I had known a man who got catfished before. He gave the woman he "fell in love with" $7,000. He never met her in person, nor saw her on a face to face app like Zoom. He only talked to her on the phone and exchanged pictures. He never heard from her again after he gave her the $7 grand. I didn't want that to happen to me but I still didn't know what I wanted.

My therapist set me straight. "Make a list. What are the qualities you want in a man? Do you care if he has kids? Do you care if he smokes or drinks? What if he doesn't have a car or a job?" she told me. "Well, I would like him to be handsome, have a nice smile, nice teeth, taller than me, maybe 5'10." Local, maybe 200 pounds. I don't want a skinny guy." I rattled off. "So, your qualities are all about his physical features. What if he looks exactly like you want him to but has the same behavior and characteristics as the men you were with in the past?" she quizzed me. "No way, oh hell no, Doctor. That scares me," I said. "You have to be clear about your intentions," she said. There it was, intentions.

In my early life... holoholo, jus' cruising. I needed to take back my life into my own hands and not allow some "rando" guy to drag me along in his direction. "If you don't know where you're going, any road will get you there," [5] pretty much summed up my life up to that point and was the lesson that the Cheshire Cat was trying to teach Alice in Wonderland:[6]

'Cheshire Puss' she began, rather timidly, as she did not at all know whether it would like the name; however, it only grinned a little wider. 'Come, it's pleased so far.' Thought Alice, and she went on. 'Would you tell me, please, which way I ought to go from here?'

'That depends a good deal on where you want to get to.' said the Cat

'I don't much care where- -'said Alice.

'Then it doesn't matter which way you go.' said the Cat.

'- -so long as I get somewhere,' Alice added as an explanation.

'Oh, you're sure to do that,' said the Cat, 'if you only walk long enough.'

My life's mission was to teach the Hawaiian language and culture and for it to flourish for future generations forever. I didn't

5   Carroll, Alice's Adventures in Wonderland, 1865.

6   Ibid #7

understand why intentions were so important until I heard Oprah talk about it with author, Gary Zukov:[7]

"This is what everybody needs to know who's on the path of spiritually opening yourself up, awakening is that it's difficult, it's challenging when you say I wanna grow, I want to be better than I have known myself to be. So, I used to have the disease to please and INTENTION cured me. So shortly after I'd read the chapter on intention, I got a call from a very famous celebrity who was asking me to do something for them and to be a part of a benefit, and I really didn't want to do it. But I thought well if I don't do it this person is gonna think I'm not a nice person. This person is gonna think I'm a selfish person. This person is gonna think, "Well, why wouldn't you do it for me?" I was thinking if I don't do it then the person is never gonna want to do anything for me if I ever call on them again and I sat with that and realized not one single response to being asked had anything to do with, "Do I really want to give of myself, my time, and my attention?" I realized in that moment that my disease to please had always been about wanting people to think I was a certain way. So I said, "no." The world did not fall apart. The person didn't hate me afterwards. Because of that I got the courage to say no again, and again, and again, and so now I only do what I intend to do. So I am here because I really want to be here, and that's when you can give of yourself fully."

That was my new word, INTENTION. So I asked myself because it was time for me to get out of the holoholo phase. "Hey you, what's your intention?"

Glossary of Chapter 13

1. Holoholo – (HOE-LOW-HOE-LOW) (def#1) "code word" or word with a hidden meaning explaining some type of activity

7 YouTube "Super Soul Sunday" https://www.youtube.com/watch?v=4iaqs4_xePk

like fishing or collecting plants/flowers from the mountain without saying the actual word itself;[8] (def#2) also means a pleasurable trip

2. Ma uka – (MA-OO-KAH) at/toward the mountains
3. Cruise – Slang for ride around aimlessly, to hang out

---

8   Definition explained to me by my Aunty Maile

CHAPTER 14

HULI KA NAʻAU; TO CHANGE FROM THE INSIDE OUT

Huli* means to change, ka is "the," and naʻau* means the innards or guts. Therefore "huli ka naʻau"* means to change from the inside or is the change coming from deep within. That was the name of the Hawaiian cover for the song "Beauty and the Beast," that Kaipoʻi Kelling and I translated. The live-action version came out in 2017 and I decided to do that song because of my previous success from the "Moana" movie.

Several months earlier, I did a Hawaiian cover version of the song "How Far I'll Go," from "Moana." My cover got over 1 million hits on Facebook and garnered tons of positive feedback. It was the first time, that I know of, that anyone translated a song into Hawaiian and did a cover version from a major movie. I worked hard on that project. I called the song, "E Kahiki e." It was so popular that the day after I posted it, it was featured on a local news channel, Hawaiʻi News Now.

The "Moana" video was a project that cost a lot and took a lot of time. Mahalo* (thanks) to all the people who helped me on this project (see mahalo section) and of course to all my fans &

friends who downloaded the song on iTunes. After my cover song came out, Disney decided to do a Hawaiian version of the Moana movie. I felt as though it was a great win and gained much-deserved exposure for ʻōlelo Hawaiʻi. I'd like to think that my cover and the positive feedback it got was the reason they decided to make the Hawaiian version.

After "Moana" people asked me to do more Hawaiian songs. I decided to cover "Beauty and the Beast." At the time, there were some kānaka who objected. They were concerned with the "Hawaiianization" or "Hawaiianizing" Disney songs. The argument was valid. Why not take a story from Hawaiian history, a moʻolelo, and do a song based on a Hawaiian story? Today it gives me pause. I didn't consider it back then because I had already made up my mind. Just recently, I read an article by the late Professor, Dr. Sam Noʻeau Warner, whom I had the privilege of taking classes from at UH. He shared their point of view. He explained it in his article on kuleana:[1]

"The Hawaiian language should be perpetuated because it is part of Hawaiian heritage-what can help to make Hawaiians whole again as a people. Hawaiians need to learn and know their language, culture, stories, histories, and religion because they interrelate and are integrally linked to one another and to the people. Language-the words people use to describe their environment, thoughts, emotions-as an expression of worldview is a medium through which people transmit culture and history. Language, separated from the environment it evolved to describe, and the thoughts and emotions that grew in that environment, becomes something new and different. The Hawaiian language taught and learned out of context, distinct from the culture (i.e., its people), becomes a new language that evolved from the original. And

---

1 Jstor.org "Kuleana, Warner" https://www.jstor.org/stable/3195982?read-now=1&seq=1#page_scan_tab_contents

although all living languages change, they usually change through evolution relative to their own people. It is my purpose to perpetuate the Hawaiian language linked to the culture of Hawaiians. As such, what is important is that the language is perpetuated among its own people, in its own cultural context and environment. There is no question that indigenous peoples can survive without their indigenous heritage languages, cultures or histories, as they have, thus far, in the United States. But they do so at a cost. Native peoples are relegated to the lower echelons of the dominant society, with low self-esteem, cut off from their pasts and their identities. Thus, when a non-Hawaiian says that Hawaiian should be saved because of its value, the question is, "value to whom?" What is the value of a people's identity?"

I needed Kaipoʻi to kōkua* (help) me. I was working on the "Beauty and the Beast" translation. I still was having trouble finding the right Hawaiian words for the title. I had looked for all kinds of words for "beauty" and "beast." For whatever reason, it was not working. I had gotten so irked because I couldn't find the right phrasing. It had to fit into 5 syllables to fit the song, "beau-ty-and-the-beast." I thought of the words "naʻauao"* (enlightened) and "naʻaupō"* (darkened). The only thing was that naʻauao, naʻaupō did not fit for the title because it was six syllables, "na-ʻau-ao-na-ʻau-pō." I needed it to be five.

That night while I slept, I had a moeʻuhane. I saw the vision of a baby living in her mom's womb. It was dark and the baby needed that darkness to grow. My kūpuna showed me that darkness was necessary and good. Seeing the "dark" or the "darkness" as bad was a foreign mindset, a haole (def#2) mindset. "Maybe seeing the dark as bad was a racist terminology created by white people who were prejudiced," I thought. "Maybe they said that darkness was bad because they were using it as a tool to oppress blacks, browns, and other people of color," I thought. Whatever it was, I woke up more frustrated than when I went to sleep. "If you guys are gonna gimme a dream please gimme a translation too," I said.

The next day, I texted Kaipo'i. Up to that point, for most of my life, I was independent. I saw asking for help as a weakness rather than a strength. I was learning that to change, to heal, to grow, I needed people. I needed help, and I needed to ask for it. He agreed to help me on one condition. He said, "Whatever Hawaiian words I use, you have to keep it, and not change it." I agreed, and we talked about the title. He asked, "Why do you want it to have two contrasting words, Beauty/Beast? Why can't it mean to change from the inside?" I said, "I like contrasting words, like "tall" and "short." "Why not use the meaning of how someone changes from the inside, and then becomes a better person on the out-side," he explained. That made sense to me. I needed to look at it with a Hawaiian mindset and perspective. Hawaiian stories always had meaning. Very rarely did they focus on superficial beauty, but rather on qualities like hard work, discipline, loyalty, family, etc. He said, "How about hu-li-ka-na-'au, five syllables. Change from the inside, because true change comes from the inside out, never from the outside in." 'Ā 'oia* (truth)!

We finished the translation. After the song was recorded, we started on the music video. I asked my friends and family to help. It was a very big project. I couldn't pay them and I felt bad and some-what guilty about it. I always bought food and drinks for everybody though. That's a local custom kinda like a potluck, where everyone brings food and doesn't come empty-handed. I always go out of my way to repay people for their help, even if I cannot give them money. When I asked, they all came to help. I was so grateful.

The lesson I learned from "Huli ka Na'au" was on giving and receiving. I consider myself a giver. Whenever somebody asks, boom! I'm there. Receiving, on the other hand, is not so easy, even when people want to help me. I feel guilty sometimes. But, it was my turn to receive. I had to remind myself that I wasn't taking, I was receiving. People wanted to help me. It was my turn.

I was blown away by all the wonderful people who helped me (see mahalo section). For years, I was declaring, "I was in the right place, at the right time, with the right people, because I AM the right people." Yet I made that declaration but acted like I didn't need people or need help from anybody. I had a big ego filled with a lot of pride. My kūpuna had to teach me again.

Once the song was pau* (finished), I became restless. "What now?" I thought. I did not want to work at the hotel anymore. It was a dead-end job. I wanted to teach Hawaiian, but I left the DOE (Department of Education) years ago and didn't know where to begin. I looked through the teacher openings. There were no Hawaiian teaching positions available so I applied for a special education (sped) teacher position at several schools. I didn't have any experience but I was just trying to get my foot back in the door. I got two callbacks, one for a job in town and another for a job in Waialua. I called Bryson and asked him, "Don't you live in Waialua?" "Yes, I do," he said. "I have a job interview down there," I said. I had just recently met him, so I didn't want to ask him for any favors. "With who?" he asked. "The principal," I said. "Christine? I know her personally. No worry sis, I got you," he told me. "Ok, mahalo," I said.

The next week I went to the school and I was greeted warmly by everyone in the office, the principal, the two office clerks, and another teacher. They were all standing up and smiling at me. "Bryson told us a lot about you," they said. Christine told me, "I loved your Beauty and the Beast video. Bryson came here and showed it to all of us. We need a Hawaiian teacher, we haven't had Hawaiian here in years. Now, I know you don't have experience teaching sped, but I'm going to hire you. You're the only one who applied, so I'm hiring you as a sped teacher, but don't worry. I'll put you into a sped teaching line and the other sped teachers will help you with your paperwork. But we want to strengthen our arts program, and I think you will be a great fit. I want you to teach a music class, can you do that, with 'ukulele? The students already chose their classes for this coming year, but I will make an announcement during the 1st week of school and open up a Hawaiian language 1st-year class. In the coming years, we will offer Hawaiian language 2nd, 3rd, and 4th year to the high schoolers." She said. "Um, yes, yah, of course. Oh my gosh," I stuttered. "Welcome to Waialua," she said.

I was ecstatic. I was yelling out the window, laughing, and crying like a crazy woman on the way home. What just happened? Not qualified, no job opening for a Hawaiian teacher, no sped experience, but I got the job? I was going to teach sped, music, and HAWAIIAN! I told Bryson the news, I think I was screaming the whole time on the phone.

I settled down on the drive back home up through Wahiawā. I heard it, "Write music. Open doors. You were in the right place, at the right time, with the right people. Music got you to the right people. You are the right people." Mental note, the next time your kūpuna tell you to do something, do it quickly. I'm so grateful for the way everything turned out. So many people helped me and believed in me. I could never have done it without them. Mahalo nui* (many thanks)!

Glossary of Chapter 14

1. Huli – (WHO-LEE) To turn or to change

2. Ka – (KAH) the Hawaiian word for "the"

3. Naʻau – (NAH-OW) innards or guts, insides, heart or affections

4. Huli ka naʻau – (WHO-LEE-KAH-NAH-OW) to change from the inside, the name of Hawaiian cover of Beauty and the Beast[2]

5. Mahalo – (MA-HAH-LOH) thanks, thank you

6. Ipu – (EEY-POO) a gourd, used sometimes as a Hawaiian musical percussion instrument accompanying chants or hula

7. Kōkua – (KOH-KOO-AH) assistance, to help

8. Naʻauao – (NAH-OW-OW) enlightened, literally means daylight mind[3]

9. Naʻaupō – (NAH-OW-POW) darkened, literally means dark mind[4]

10. ʻĀ ʻoia – (AH-OH-YA) certainly, truth

11. Pau – (PAH-OOH) finished, end

12. Mahalo nui – (MA-HAH-LOH-NOO-EEY) thanks a lot, idiom meaning thank you very much

---

2   YouTube "Huli Ka Naʻau" https://www.youtube.com/watch?v=tuDKdOlkPcQ

3   Wehewehe wikiwiki https://hilo.hawaii.edu/wehe/?q=naauao

4   Wehewehe wikiwiki https://hilo.hawaii.edu/wehe/?q=naaupo

CHAPTER 15

KŪ KIAʻI MAUNA; WE ARE MAUNAKEA

The Maunakea* (sacred mountain on the island of Hawaiʻi) Movement, also known as Kū Kiaʻi Mauna* (Protectors of Maunakea) and We Are Maunakea (the hashtag started by the actor Jason Momoa - #wearemaunakea), is the movement to stop the Thirty Meter Telescope Organization (TMT) from building the largest tele-scope in the world on the Maunakea mountain top. In this cen-tury, there has never been an issue that has unified the people of Hawaiʻi, galvanized Hawaiians and non-Hawaiians alike to action, and informed the rest of the world of injustices done (and still being done) by Hawaiʻi's state government.

The movement started by kiaʻi* (protectors), is founded on the belief that the Mauna* (mountain) is sacred to native Hawaiians. It is the piko* (or center) of Hawaiʻi Island. It is known in ancient chants to be the offspring of Wākea and Papahānaumoku.[1] The name of the Mauna is Maunakea. or Mauna a Wākea.*

The organization called Puʻuhonua o Puʻuhuluhulu was birthed from the struggle. Their website, puuhuluhulu.com, states that "Puʻuhonua o Puʻuhuluhulu was established by kiaʻi with the

---

1   Ka Nupepa Kuokoa March 24, 1866 https://www.papakilodatabase.com/pdnupepa/cgi-bin/pdnupepa?a=d&d=KNK18660324-01.2.27&e=-------en-20--1--txt-txIN%7ctx-NU%7ctxTR--------

support of the Royal Order of Kamehameha ʻEkahi for the purpose of protecting sacred Maunakea."[2]

In 2009, Maunakea was chosen by TMT as the site of the massive telescope because of the high altitude and pristine climate. The kiaʻi resisted, protesting and blocking the start of its construction in 2015. Lawsuits were filed to stop construction. Yet despite the people's concerns, the University of Hawaiʻi, the managing authority, pushed to have it built.

TMT is not the first telescope to be built on Maunakea. Currently, the summit of Maunakea is home to 13 other telescopes. Gross negligence was documented in the video "50 years of mismanaging Mauna Kea" since the construction of the first telescope in 1967[3].

After all of those years of inaction and neglect, the State of Hawaiʻi continues to entrust the University of Hawaiʻi with stewardship over Maunakea. They say in their most recent video[4] on the UH website that they are taking steps to correct their mistakes. I liken this to a parent who lets someone abuse his daughter over and over, knowing full well the damage it is causing her. Yet because he has no aloha or concern for her well-being does nothing to step in to protect her. Who then is responsible to remove her from that situation when they, who are supposed to take care of her, do nothing to stop the abuse?

We are taught to mālama* (to care for) our kūpuna. It is a value that is entwined in our history. Thirty-eight kūpuna were arrested on Maunakea on July 17, 2019, for blocking the Ala Hulu Kūpuna* (Maunakea access road) in order to halt construction of the

---

2   Puʻuhonua o Puʻuhuluhulu https://www.puuhuluhulu.com/

3   50 years of mismanaging Mauna Kea https://www.youtube.com/watch?v=H-MumZ-InUvs

4   UH stewardship of Maunakea https://www.hawaii.edu/maunakea-stewardship/

TMT[5]. There was so much public outrage at the state for making DOCARE (Division of Conservation and Resources Enforcement) officers, most of whom are locals and family members, neighbors, and friends arrest our kūpuna. Aunty Maxine Kahaʻulelio, one of the thirty-eight arrested, tells about the kiaʻi meeting prior to the arrest: [6]

"We had a meeting, with some people you know and at this meeting I told (Kahoʻokahi) Kanuha no you're not getting arrested, you are not getting arrested, none of you are getting arrested, I'm going to get arrested and my friend Gwen Kim going get, and my other friend going get arrested because you know what, my life almost pau (finished) so now is my time to stand up for you folks, because no more of our young ones, no more, no more, they have family they have their future, they got their jobs, I pau already, I'm retired, I have my own hale (house), 'nuff, let me do my part as a kanaka maoli* (native Hawaiian)."

Kapu* (restraint, restricted) aloha* (humility, love) is the strategy that kiaʻi have been using in this battle. It is "an evolving, philosophical code of conduct that is culturally informed by kanaka maoli ontologies and epistemologies, being expressed politically through non-violent direct action, and ceremonially through behavioral conduct in alignment with kanaka maoli cultural practices and notions of the sacred."[7] Doctor, Hawaiian activist, native, historian, teacher, cultural practitioner, kumu hula* (hula teacher) Aunty Pua Kanahele, explains it this way:[8]

"Kapu aloha has two English definitions that are usually used. One word is prohibited and the other word is sacred. In the case

---

5   Hawaii News Now https://www.hawaiinewsnow.com/2019/09/21/kupuna-who-were-arrested-tmt-protest-july-plead-not-guilty-obstruction/

6   YouTube "Like a mighty wave" https://www.youtube.com/watch?time_continue=164&v=4J3ZCzHMMPQ&feature=emb_logo

7   Wikipedia definition https://en.wikipedia.org/wiki/Kapu_Aloha

8   Puuhuluhulu.com "Kapu aloha" https://www.puuhuluhulu.com/learn/kapualoha

of kapu aloha, it means both and the idea of the way you behave should be sacred to not only yourself but the people around you, prohibited because you're prohibited to act in a certain way. The aloha part has many different meanings one of the greater meanings that everybody uses as aloha is love. You can use love in many different ways, and love is many different levels of acceptance. You know you have the love between a mother and a daughter, a mother and children, you have a love between a husband and wife, you have a love between cousins, you have a love between friends, and then you have a love between people you meet for this first time and you have a good relationship with them, and by the time you've talked for a few days, you tell a person, "I love you." So when we talk about kapu aloha we're talking about a prohibition, a way to act, with the idea of exuding a particular level of love."

Police were everywhere. The State put up signs shortly after the conflict started fronting the main highway that said, "No parking, stopping, standing, loading, and unloading." It angered people and "definitely seems like a form of harassment though, as they could choose to do this anywhere in the island or across the state, but they have chosen to target kiai and the puuhonua for petty things that in another situation or in other areas most likely would not be cited,"[9] said Kahoʻokahi Kanuha.

Hawaiʻi's Governor Ige was flooding the airwaves with false claims and lies.[10] He bad-mouthed the kiaʻi saying that supporters up at the Mauna were drinking, taking drugs, and smoking pot. Police presence was beefed up on and around the Mauna. In the span of one month from July to August 2019, police set up checkpoints along the 52-mile stretch of Daniel K. Inouye Highway (the

---

9   Hawaii News Now https://www.hawaiinewsnow.com/2019/08/20/dot-installs-no-parking-signs-mauna-kea/

10 Khon2 https://www.khon2.com/local-news/kiai-calls-ige-a-liar-after-he-made-claims-of-alleged-illegal-activity/

road fronting Maunakea). Hundreds of tickets and citations were handed out in what were intimidation and harassment tactics.[11]

Over a month after the arrests as the standoff continued to gain momentum, a wooden structure was erected in the lava field on the opposite side of the kūpuna camp* (site of the protests). It was slated to be a children's learning center site. The state deemed it an "illegal" and "unpermitted" structure.[12] On September 6, 2019, state police and a construction crew came to tear it down. Hawai'i News Now (HNN) reported:[13]

"Before an illegal structure was removed from Mauna kea on Friday, an officer used a chainsaw to cut through a boarded up door to make sure no one was inside. In doing so, he also cut through a Hawaiian flag affixed to the door. And that action quickly drew condemnation from protesters, who said the action amounted to desecration and could have easily been avoided. The flag had been affixed to the structure before demolition crews arrived. On Friday morning, HNN saw activists using nails or screws to affix the flag to the structure's entrance. Plywood was also bolted to the door while a window was covered from the inside. Activist leaders say the flag was tacked on and mounted for display. Shortly afterward, law enforcement and state Transportation Department crews moved in. In video shot at the protest camp, a law enforcement officer can be seen cutting into the structure and leaving the Hawaiian flag cut and torn. "The first thing that they did was slice that Hawaiian flag right in half and that served only to agitate and escalate the emotions of the people who were there," said TMT protester Andre Perez.

11 Hawaii News Now https://www.hawaiinewsnow.com/2019/08/23/hawaii-county-police-hand-out-citations-mauna-kea-frustration-mounts/

12 Hawaii News Now https://www.hawaiinewsnow.com/video/2019/09/04/unpermitted-wooden-structure-going-up-mauna-kea-base-camp-state-not-protestors-could-face-fines/

13 H https://www.hawaiinewsnow.com/2019/09/07/state-draws-heat-how-hawaiian-flag-was-handled-protesters-structure/

Governor Ige reported that the officer sawed through the flag on the door because he could not see inside the structure. Later that day pictures surfaced of the glass window on the side of the door with a clear view inside of the building. The governor had misspoken or lied. Many believed that the state was using gaslighting and cointelpro tactics. They disrespected the flag, trying to incite people to go crazy and attack them. The state knew the outrage that people would feel watching them disrespect the Hawaiian flag. If their tactic worked and people revolted, the state would be able to use force and arrest kia'i. That would quash the growing movement. That tactic backfired because most everyone remained in kapu aloha, and only two men who revolted were arrested that day.

After that, a video surfaced alleging police misconduct. It was a video recording of an officer who was unaware that he was being recorded. He was supposedly giving false information of the flag cutting: "leaders of the protests on Mauna Kea, are calling for a federal investigation into the state's enforcement of Thirty Meter Telescope opponents and asking for the removal of a Hawaii County police officer who they said spread misinformation. Protesters released a video statement Tuesday alleging that the state is using enforcement tactics that "harass, intimidate, and vilify Mauna Kea protectors." They provided a list of so-called "questionable" law enforcement actions, including the use of sobriety checkpoints, more vehicles parked in and around the blockade, and complaints of high beams and a low-flying helicopter over the kupuna camp. They also provided the media with video and audio evidence of what they allege is a Hawaii County police officer providing false information to Mauna kea protester Michael Glendon "in an apparent attempt to provoke him to retaliate against two supposed informants in our puuhonua." [14]

14 YouTube "TMT protestors seek probe of alleged police misconduct" https://www.youtube.com/watch?v=IfEH2832TS4

As the policing of the state became more aggressive, the movement gained more support. People like Jason Momoa and the Rock, Duane Johnson, visited the Mauna and spoke out on behalf of the movement. It was history in the making as thousands walked through Waikīkī[15] showing their support. It was the first of many demonstrations.[16]

Mauna convoys started up also where hundreds of cars showed their unity.[17] People were asked to fly their Hawaiian flags to show their support. I saw no less than ten cars per day with flags flying from trucks, cars, vans, trailers, and big rigs. People had flags stuck to their side window, antenna, tailgates, truck flag-poles, pole racks, everywhere. Shortly thereafter, the state started ticketing people for their flags. HPD (Honolulu Police Department) Deputy Chief John McCarthy said, "motorists were cited for violating a state law prohibiting obstruction while driving and were not selectively handed tickets."[18]

Andrea Freeman, a UH law professor sited some serious First Amendment concerns, "The way I view the situation is completely one of harassment and oppression... The idea that this is about obstructing traffic or safety is really just a pretext because it's not something that we've seen consistently. You know, protectors are on the mauna and more protectors are gathering. I think this is a backlash to that. She said similar concerns were raised on the Big Island when authorities began erecting "no parking" signs along the Daniel K. Inouye Highway at Mauna Kea Access Road where a protest continues against construction of the Thirty Meter

---

15 Kitv4 https://www.kitv.com/story/40816557/thousands-march-through-waikiki-against-tmt

16 Khon2 https://www.khon2.com/local-news/more-than-10000-march-through-waikiki-to-support-mauna-kea-and-the-protection-of-hawaiian-lands/

17 Kitv4 https://www.kitv.com/story/41018559/hundreds-of-mauna-kea-protectors-led-convoy-from-hawaii-kai-to-waianae

18 Hawaii Public Radio https://www.hawaiipublicradio.org/post/why-hawaiian-flags-parking-tickets-arrests-are-raising-free-speech-questions#stream/0

Telescope… UH professor Freeman said flags in particular have a history as symbols that are valued, cherished, and respected. Whether it's being used for free speech because you want to burn a flag or because you want to fly a flag, your rights are protected either way."[19]

Some say that the reason why a majority of people support the movement is because of all the injustices done to the Hawaiian people. That may be true, but it's still all about the care and proper stewardship of Maunakea. How much longer do we have to endure disrespect, abuse, and bad stewardship over our land?

I watched in horror as a video on Facebook surfaced of the thirty-eight kūpuna arrested on Maunakea for blocking TMT construction. It shook me to my core. Watching all of them arrested like criminals as the police zip tied the hands of our old people. I watched as the natives of this land were shuffled, wheeled, and carried out to police vans. People wailed, chanted, and cried, but remained kūpaʻa* (steadfast). The kūpuna gave me the courage to believe that our elders, those past and present are to be trusted to guide our steps.

When the events unfolded in July 2019, it was history in the making and I knew I had to go to the Mauna. I called my parents and told them that I wanted to go. I was proud that my mom had been going regularly to support and participate with her hula ʻohana of Mauna a Wākea. My whole family had gone including my daughter Hoʻoli who flew to Hawaiʻi Island to go there. I finally made it back home almost two months later. My dad and I were planning to head

19 Ibid #16

up on September 6, 2019. On that day the Hawaiian flag cutting incident happened so we decided not to go up.

We went up the next day. We supported the movement by bringing some food that we had made, two large pans of shoyu chicken, and one large pan of white rice. We attended some classes, and took a walking tour. It was an unprecedented day in history. We stood in solidarity as leaders on the Mauna held a press conference. The speakers were Hawaiian Homestead residents Aunty Pua Kanahele, Kaleikoa Kaeo, and Halealoha Ayau.

My dad made a profound statement at the end of that day. I watched him quietly hobble around in pain. He had just recently had knee surgery and had a hard time standing for long periods of time. Informational classes were happening, Mauna run classes, at "Pu'u huluhulu University." We walked from class to class stopping to listen for a few minutes each. He kept rubbing his knee as he limped around. We took a one-hour walking tour up to the top of Pu'u huluhulu. A young kanaka guided us up as he talked about the protocols, the significance of the area, the native plants, and the animals. When we finally got to the top of the Pu'u, we walked over to the end of the hill. We stood next to the ground stake that held the upside-down Hawaiian flag. We asked the guy behind us to take our picture with the flag, and shortly after my dad said, "I never seen anything like this in my lifetime. I am proud to be Hawaiian." Me too dad, me too.

The kapu aloha that people have held themselves to all this time is commendable. People in Hawai'i are proud, proud of our heritage, and proud of our Hawaiian flag. It is a symbol of the monarchy, as that was the flag of the Hawaiian kingdom before the overthrow. The flag flies today as the State of Hawai'i flag. To be proud of our flag simply means just that, we are proud. It means no disrespect to America. People who get offended at Hawaiian loyalty must realize that Hawai'i was a country before the over-throw. The hurt that was done to our Hawaiian nation, though I was not alive at the time, still hurts me and others who were affected by the events of the past. My ancestors who were alive during the overthrow lived through the hurt. They passed the hurt to my kūpuna, and their hurts are alive, flowing through my body in my blood, and in my DNA. The hurt will remain until restitution, healing, and justice is served.

As I write this chapter , I cry. I cry thinking of the videos, pictures, and articles of the kūpuna arrests. The wounds go deep. It stirred up memories of the abuse of Hawai'i, her queen, her people, and her overthrow over 125 years ago. As I cry, I hear the haunting lyrics in the song "Hawaii '78" written by Mickey Ioane and sung by the Mākaha Sons[20]. The melody haunts my ears:

Ua mau ke ea o ka 'āina i ka pono o Hawai'i

(The sovereignty of the land is perpetuated in righteousness) – author's note: ea is translated as sovereignty

If just for a day our king and queen

Would visit all these islands and saw everything

How would they feel about the changes of our land

Could you just imagine if they were around

And saw highways on their sacred grounds

How would they feel about this modern city life

Tears would come from each other's eyes

As they would stop to realize

That our people are in great, great danger now

How would they feel, would their smiles be content, then cry?

---

20 YouTube "Hawaii '78" https://www.youtube.com/watch?v=LGEHPRtBln8

Cry for the gods, cry for the people

Cry for the land that was taken away

And then yet you'll find, Hawai'i

Could you just imagine if they came back

And saw traffic lights and railroad tracks

How would they feel about this modern city life

Tears would come from each other's eyes

As they would stop to realize

That our land is in great, great danger now

All the fighting that the king has done

To conquer all these islands now there's condominiums

How would he feel if he saw Hawai'i nei

How would he feel, would his smile be content, then cry

Glossary of Chapter 15

1. Maunakea – (MA-OO-NAH-KAY-AH) sacred mountain on Hawai'i, source of most of the islands water supply

2. Kū Kia'i Mauna – (KOO-KEY-AH-EEY-MA-OO-NAH) Protectors of Maunakea; the Maunakea Movement to stop the Thirty Meter Telescope from being built on the summit of Maunakea

3. Kū – (KOO) to stand

4. Kia'i – (KEY-AH-EEY) protector/protectors [singular/plural]

5. Mauna – (MA-OO-NAH) Mountain

6. Piko – (PEE-KOH-OO) Center

7. Mauna a Wākea – (MA-OO-NAH-AH-WAH-KAY-AH) Mountain of Wākea, another name for Maunakea

8. Mālama – (MA-LAH-MA) to care for

9. Ala hulu kūpuna – (AH-LAH-WHO-LOO-KOO-POO-NAH) Maunakea access road

10. Kanaka maoli – (KAH-NAH-KAH-MA-OO-LEE) native Hawaiians

11. Kapu – (KAH-POO) restraint, prohibited

12. Kapu aloha – (KAH-POO-AH-LOH-HAH) use of nonviolent restraint of one's self toward adversaries

13. Kumu hula – (KOO-MOO-WHO-LAH) hula teacher

14. Kūpuna camp – KOO-POO-NAH) site of the protests

15. Kūpaʻa – (KOO-POO-NAH) steadfast

CHAPTER 16

KA LEO HAWAIʻI; HAWAIIAN, MY FIRST LANGUAGE

By the 1970s, the Hawaiian Language was dying. The kūpuna knew it and by that time there was a language gap. The kūpuna were able to speak their ʻōlelo, but because they didn't speak to their children, their children didn't ʻōlelo Hawaiʻi. They knew that it was in danger of becoming extinct. An article called, "Saving the Hawaiian Language" explains the dilemma:[1]

"Eighty nine years later, in 1985, only 32 island children under the age of 18 – including the keiki (children) on the island of Niʻihau – spoke the language.

During that decade the grandchildren of the last generation of native speakers (kūpuna) chose to begin revitalizing their native language and culture by teaching their children Hawaiian. Recognizing that higher education was not producing fluent or near fluent Hawaiian speakers, they started the immersion education movement to make Hawaiian ʻŌlelo a living language once again.

It takes one generation to lose a language and three generations to recover it. The Hawaiian language renaissance is in the

---

1   University of Hawaiʻi Foundation https://www.uhfoundation.org/saving-hawaiian-language

middle of the second generation. The language is still endangered but the growing number of native speakers is encouraging. As one of the immersion movement founders describes it: "Our numbers are hope."

The 2010 census reported that 24,000 households identified Hawaiian as their dominant language. A handful of children in the first Hawaiian immersion classes in the 1980s has grown to more than 2,500 students annually enrolled in the 11 preschool and 21 immersion and charter school sites. Another 8,000 study Hawaiian language in other higher education settings each year."

In 1972, a young professor at UH Mānoa named Larry Kimura, started hosting a radio show with mānaleo and interviewed them in their native language. He estimated that there were only about 2,000 people left who grew up speaking Hawaiian in their home. The program was called, "Ka Leo Hawai'i*" (the Hawaiian voice). He had to convince the station to air the program because, "hearing Hawaiians talk to each other on the radio in their own language was radical at the time."[2] Today, he is called the "grandfather" of the Hawaiian language because his radio show helped spark the revival of the language.

One of his students, Keiki Kawai'ae'a, now the director for the College of Hawaiian Language at UH also pushed to reclaim the language. "The '70s is really part of that whole Hawaiian renaissance… We were part of the generation where women were burning their bras, and civil rights, and people were asking, "How come I can't speak the language of my grandparents? How come they had this and I don't have that?" she said.[3]

2   Npr.org https://www.npr.org/sections/codeswitch/2019/06/22/452551172/the-hawaiian-language-nearly-died-a-radio-show-sparked-its-revival

3   Ibid #2

In an article about language extinction and culture, author Amy Hunt explains what happens to a culture when a language dies:[4]

"Cultural knowledge and identity are inextricably wound up in language. According to UNESCO, "Every language reflects a unique world-view with its own value systems, philosophy and particular cultural features. The extinction of a language results in the irrecoverable loss of unique cultural knowledge embodied in it for centuries, including historical, spiritual and ecological knowledge that may be essential for the survival of not only its speakers, but also countless others.""

When a language belonging to people in the Amazon dies, so too does that people's knowledge of the rainforest, how they discuss and interpret certain aspects of how to live in and with that environment, the uses for plants that may still be unknown to the rest of the world, and the words for smells and colors that other cultures and languages can't distinguish...

Knowledge of and connection to the world isn't the only aspect of culture that language is intimately tied to: language forms a critical aspect of a person's and a community's identity as well. Dr. Pamela Serota discussed language loss and identity with the Atlantic: "Because language discloses cultural and historical meaning, the loss of language is a loss of that link to the past. Without a link to the past, people in a culture lose a sense of place, purpose and path: one must know where one came from to know where one is going. The loss of language undermines a people's sense of identity and belonging, which uproots the entire community in the end." A person's mother tongue is the first means they have of communicating with their family and their peers about the world around them, their heritage and belief systems. Though

4   Culture Ready http://www.cultureready.org/blog/language-extinction-and-what-means-culture

they may learn and speak other languages, the loss of their mother tongue is the loss of a personal connection to what and who came before them, and an inability to pass that heritage on to the next generation."

The only way to stop it from going extinct is to use it and to teach it. In 1978, Hawai'i became an official language of Hawai'i, alongside English. Article XV, Section 4 states, "English and Hawaiian shall be the official languages of Hawai'i, except that Hawaiian shall be required for public acts and transactions only as provided by law."[5] In theory, this is great. But in practice, it's not. In my opinion, the Hawai'i Department of Education should require at least one to two years of Hawaiian language in high school for every student. It should be a state requirement to learn the "official language." That would not make up for the 1896 law[6] banning Hawaiian in school, but that would be a gesture of reparations and of goodwill toward the Hawaiian race.

I define language as the pocket that holds culture. It also holds words, values, and traditions. Like Kaipo'i said, "when you learn another language or you learn your own language, it opens another door, another way for you to look at the world. But also this is the only place in the world where Hawaiian is the home language."[7]

5   Capitol https://www.capitol.hawaii.gov/hrscurrent/Vol01_Ch0001-0042F/05-Const/CONST_0015-0004.htm

6   Hawaii State Department of Education http://www.hawaiipublicschools.org/TeachingAndLearning/StudentLearning/HawaiianEducation/Pages/History-of-the-Hawaiian-Education-program.aspx#:~:text=After%20the%20overthrow%20of%20the,-for%20the%20next%20four%20generations.

7   YouTube "Why Hawaiian is not the main language of Hawaii, Kaipo'i Kelling" https://www.youtube.com/watch?v=v7rWe78J5iA

My daughter, Hiʻilani, attended a Hawaiian immersion public school. A Hawaiian immersion school is where students speak in Hawaiian as their communication language. She attended immersion since preschool until she was in the 6th grade. The teachers speak in Hawaiian to them and teach them all subject areas through the medium of the Hawaiian Language. She speaks Hawaiian conversationally and fluently.

I also speak Hawaiian conversationally and fluently. As I mentioned, I learned Hawaiian in college at the University of Hawaiʻi at Mānoa, where I got a professional diploma in Hawaiian language. Because both Hiʻilani and I speak Hawaiian, my mom and I had a conversation about our native language.

During that discussion, my mom asked me why I don't speak Hawaiian to my daughter more often every day. The first reason, or maybe excuse that I gave her, was that it is much easier to speak English to her because English is my first language and the first language that I learned growing up. The second reason was that I am not a mānaleo (native speaker of Hawaiian). Besides that, I told her that it is just easier, in general, to speak English since I speak it to most everyone else that I know, and I know more English vocabulary than Hawaiian.

Our conversation went something like this:

Mom: Why don't you speak in Hawaiian more to your daughter.

Me: Well, it's just easier to speak English to her. English is my first language.

Mom: It may be easier but what's best for the survival of the language and our people?

Me:	Well, I'm not a mānaleo and Hawaiian is <u>not</u> my first language.
Mom:	I did not ask you if you were a mānaleo. Who says Hawaiian IS NOT your first language?
Me:	Well I learned English first, and I did not speak Hawaiian growing up.
Mom:	Whose definition is that, the colonizer's definition? The people who overthrew the language? You speak Hawaiian now, because you learned it in college. It is your FIRST language because it was the language of your ancestors and the language that was FIRST here before the foreigners came and forced us to believe in their definitions and to think the way they think and believe in what they believe, in the way that they believe it. Hawaiian is in your blood, that is the language of your people. Speak Hawaiian more to your daughter and it will become your FIRST language because you will speak it FIRST, before you speak English.
Me:	Huh, I never thought of it like that. Wow, that just blows my mind. Mahalo.

Those deep words cut straight into my heart, my na'au. Who am I? What do I believe? Who am I letting write the story of my life? What narrative did I believe for so many years? The narrative of the colonizers who overthrew my queen. Do I trust them? Do I trust their language?

Glossary of Chapter 16

1. Ka Leo Hawaiʻi – (KAH-LAY-OH-HAH-WAH-EEY) the Hawaiian voice; the name of a radio program in the 70s, hosted by Larry Kimura

2. Ua – rain (OOH-AH)

CHAPTER 17

HE KANAKA; POWER TO THE PEOPLE

He Kanaka* (a person) means mankind, or a person, usually a Hawaiian man. It also can have a derogatory meaning, "In a vulgar, low sense as sometimes used by foreigners, a Hawaiian, a native, in distinction from a foreigner."[1] Kanaka have been victims of institutional (systemic racism), especially since the overthrow.

In 1893, the group that overthrew the Queen was known as the "Committee of Safety." They were made up of thirteen men. Those men were part of an elite group. Most were American, born of the Calvinist Christian missionaries who came to convert islanders to their religion, whose families had benefited and amassed great wealth by their business transactions here. After the overthrow, they asked for the help of the United States of America. The president at the time was Grover Cleveland, the 24th US President. Grover Cleveland investigated the overthrow and found that they were complicit in the "lawless overthrow of the lawful, peaceful government of Hawai'i."[2] He ordered them to give Hawai'i back to the Queen. They refused to comply with Cleveland's orders. Instead, they formed a new government. Their government was called the "Republic of Hawai'i." They chose a man named Sanford

1 Wehewehe wikiwiki https://hilo.hawaii.edu/wehe/?q=kanaka

2 Wikipedia https://en.wikipedia.org/wiki/Blount_Report

B. Dole to be their new president of the Republic. Thereafter, a new president of the US was elected. His name was William McKinley, 25th US President. McKinley annexed Hawai'i into the US, even though he knew what the Republic had done and that the overthrow was illegal. That "Treaty of Annexation" made Hawai'i a territory of the US. Those men who overthrew the queen were rich, white businessmen, and racists. They imprisoned the queen in her own home. They stripped her of her power, authority, property, and dignity.

It was hard finding books from primary sources about the real history of Hawai'i. Fortunately, Lili'uokalani wrote her history down. There is no better primary source than Hawai'i's queen. More resources written by Hawaiians, about Hawaiians, are needed. In an article by Robin Puanani Danner she writes:[3]

"It is my hope that, by next year's conference, this group will have harnessed the talent and passion of Native Hawaiian historians, of Native Hawaiian language experts, of Native Hawaiian navigators, and the elders and keepers of our rich culture, and with it, we have researched and produced the first and best high school and collegiate level textbook on Native Hawaiian history. In doing so, we will make our world accessible to our own community and the larger community that at times struggles to understand us. My own children attended public school and signed up for the American History course as well as the Hawaiian History course. I cannot tell you my dismay to find them working with a textbook for one, and a mishmash of Xerox copies for the other. We need Hawaiian history textbooks in our schools. Textbooks on us-and written by us-will make great strides in building support and understanding about our people. This single research project alone, of producing a solid educational textbook on our people, is worth

---

3   Ulukau "The Economy, a Western Tool to Achieve our Native Goals" http://ulukau. org/elib/cgi-bin/library?e=d-0hulili04-000Sec--11en-50-20-frameset-book--1-010es-capewin&a=d&d=D0.3&toc=0

hundreds of other research projects going by the wayside. I beg you to do it."

Some textbooks never mentioned the overthrow, and other texts gloss over America's role in their crime. According to teacher Umi Perkins, textbooks about Hawaiian history are sub-par. They barely mention anything and when they do, the information is incomplete. Schools need more accurate and complete textbooks. Here are what some US history textbooks say about the overthrow:[4]

- "Queen Lily was overthrown by her people" (false statement)
- President Cleveland... withdrew the annexation treaty from the Senate and tried to restore Lili'uokalani to power... Five years later, the United States annexed Hawai'i.
- Cleveland... tried to restore Queen Lil to her throne. Not until after the Spanish-American War was Hawai'i finally annexed by a joint resolution of Congress;
- In August 1898, Hawai'i was officially annexed to the United States and became the Territory of Hawai'i."

To get a clearer understanding of racism, the following words are defined below: Racism, racist, elite, systemic racism, and institutional racism. Systemic racism and institutional racism are used interchangeably as they usually mean the same thing.

- Racism:[5] "a belief or doctrine that inherent differences among the various human racial groups determine cultural or individual achievement, usually involving the idea that one's own race is superior and has the right to dominate others or that a particular racial group is inferior to others"

---

4   YouTube "Ted Talks, Umi Perkins" https://www.youtube.com/watch?v=TVsk1O8KMBI

5   Dictionary.com https://www.dictionary.com/browse/racism

- Racist:[6] "a person who believes in racism, the doctrine that one's own racial group is superior or that a particular racial group is inferior to the others."

- Elite:[7] "a group or class of people seen as having the greatest power and influence within a society, especially because of their wealth or privilege."

- Systemic racism:[8] "ongoing racial inequalities maintained by society."

- Institutional racism: def1[9]-"discriminatory policies and practices within organizations and institutions:" def2[10] -"the systematic distribution of resources, power, and opportunity in our society to the benefit of people who are white and the exclusion of people of color."

Two examples of institutional racism/systemic racism here in Hawai'i :

1. *Institutional Racism in the Justice System back then*

   The Massie Affair: The false accusal by a rich haole (def#1 & #2) woman, Thalia Massie, of rape against five poor local men: 2 Hawaiians-Joseph Kahahawai and Ben Ahakuelo, 2 Japanese–Horace Ida and David Takai; and 1 Hawaiian/ Chinese man-Henry Chang.[11]

   Thalia's husband, Lieutenant Thomas Massie was a navy man stationed on O'ahu. On September 12, 1931, they both

---

6   Dictionary.com https://www.dictionary.com/browse/racist

7   Oxford Dictionary https://www.lexico.com/en/definition/elite

8   Frank Porter Graham Child Development Institute https://fpg.unc.edu/sites/fpg.unc. edu/files/resources/other-resources/What%20Racism%20Looks%20Like.pdf

9   Ibid #6

10 Racial Equity Tools https://www.racialequitytools.org/resourcefiles/institutionalracism. pdf

11 University of Minnesota Law Library http://moses.law.umn.edu/darrow/trialpdfs/ MASSIE_CASE.pdf

were at the Ala Wai Inn, a nightspot in Honolulu. They got into an argument and Thalia left. As she was walking home, she was assaulted. Witnesses later said that they saw a big haole (def#1) man following her. She later reported the incident but could not remember the details of her assailant. There was no evidence, but five local men were rounded up for the assault. At the trial, there were many discrepancies in her testimony, and little evidence corroborating her story. Many eyewitnesses saw the five men at different locations on the night of the alleged rape, none of which was the location at which she was attacked. The case was deemed a mistrial. Thalia's mother, Grace Fortescue, was outraged. The following month, she took matters into her own hands. She, her son-in-law Thomas, and two enlisted men kidnapped Joseph Kahahawai, tortured, and killed him. They took his body to a deserted area where they planned to dispose of the body. Police were alerted to the kidnapping. They were pulled over in Fortescue's vehicle and found with the dead body of Kahahawai. They were arrested, tried, and found guilty of manslaughter rather than mur-der. Locals were enraged at the injustice. Justice was never served. Governor Lawrence M. Judd commuted the 10-year sentence for the convicted killers to 1-hour. The four sat in Governor Judd's office and had drinks with him and then they were released after an hour. Institutional racism.

2. *Institutional Racism in the Higher Education System here now*

On September 5, 2019, the Institute for Astronomy at UH Mānoa held a conference in support of TMT. During the question and answer session, UH Mānoa professor John Learned made racist statements about Hawaiians at Kamehameha School. Kamehameha School ("Kam" School is derogatory, as Kam is a Chinese word, whereas Kamehameha is a Hawaiian word) is a school that admits students of Hawaiian ancestry. Learned's statements were recorded by a faculty member of the College of Education, assistant professor, Summer Maunakea, a graduate of Kamehameha school. Statements from Learned:[12]

"We all know that the Kam Schools are academically not successful... a student who was working on his master's and is a physics teacher at Kam Schools, he told me that he had to graduate people in physics who couldn't even read."

In another post, a screenshot of an email written by Learned and sent to his colleagues is posted on the Facebook page of the group 'Onipa'a Kākou. Learned's email is filled with untruths and racist statements against kanaka. It is dated August 22, 2017, by Learned to his physics colleagues. He writes:[13]

Dear Physics Colleagues:

It is a season for action to defend science. I plan to use some class time, and I hope you will too, to tell the students about the need to stand up to this nonsense in the protestors trying to monopolize Mauna Kea. I hope our IFA friends will produce some counter propaganda, but I think we can all help our students understand that this anti-TMT activity is nonsense. There is no rational reason why the mountain top cannot be shared, as it was in the past (including Hawaiians having an industry there manufacturing flint tools). Moreover the 19th century Hawaiian Royalty were very much in favor of astronomy.

In case you did not know several important things have happened recently. The courts have found that there is no barrier to proceeding with construction, which can proceed after

---

12 Ka Leo http://www.manoanow.org/kaleo/news/uh-m-noa-professor-john-learned-apologizes-for-inappropriate-kamehameha-schools-remarks/article_6c6c3a66-dd8b-11e9-b17b-f33f83a98daa.html

13 Facebook https://www.facebook.com/onipaa125/posts/407047819953875/

DLNR approval. Maybe even more importantly several prominent Hawaiian leaders have come out in favor of the TMT (I have talked with an important Hawaiian a few years ago, who said the Mauna Kea business was all nonsense and a recent invention, but who would not speak out for fear of attack). A large majority of State citizens, Hawaiian and otherwise, support the astronomy industry on the Big Island; only a small noisy minority want to turn back the clock.

My two cents: Let me be clear that I (we all) understand the terrible thing that was done to Hawaiians more than a century ago, in stealing their land and banning their culture. There is no turning back however and we all need to move on, and to give particular respect to the earlier immigrants to the islands. No doubt Mauna kea and Haleakala are special places, for all of humanity. We should all respect and treasure those unique locations. But in no way should we go back a few centuries to a stone age culture, with a few (illegitimate) Kahunas telling everyone else how to behave.

This can all be resolved with aloha,

John

P.S. Also in discussions with people, ask about the protest leadership. For example, I think the leading lady is a former mountain top employee who was fired for cause and is not even Hawaiian. Also, ask who is supplying airline tickets and rental cars for protestors? And the large legal bills? Who stand to gain from the millions being extorted from TMT? With many it is just being suckered in by the nostalgia, anti-growth sentiment, and simmering anger from a century ago, but the behind the scenes anti-TMT leadership surely have their own axes to grind… "follow the money."

P.P.S. Last time one of our physics faculty was criticized for speaking out in class about the TMT. I heard from some (non-P&A) students that in (some of) their classes at Hawaiian studies, they were being propagandized against TMT, told some things I know to be wrong, and encouraged to get out and protest. Let us hope that Hawaiian studies faculty will be more reasonable this time.

These racist statements are not opinions held solely by Professor John Learned. This statement by kiaʻi was printed in the UH newspaper, "Ka Leo,"[14] "while Learned's behavior is deplorable, so are the behaviors of other senior faculty members whose anti-Hawaiian, anti-local rhetoric appears on emails that are archived on the UH system."

These dangerous opinions and mindsets continue today, as Professor Learned is protected by his union, UHPA. He is free to share his racist attitudes with his students because his viewpoint is immune to punishment. In 2019, an article stated that "UH condemns Learned's statements and Learned also apologized for his comments. UH has not confirmed if any disciplinary action will take place,"[15] As of the writing of this book in 2020, Learned is still employed as a faculty member at the University of Hawaiʻi at Mānoa's department of physics and astronomy.[16]

I thought I didn't know the names of the men who were part of the "Committee of Safety," but I did. Their names are alive all over Hawaiʻi represented and memorialized in street names, places, and

14 Ka Leo http://www.manoanow.org/kaleo/news/uh-m-noa-professor-john-learned-apol-ogizes-for-inappropriate-kamehameha-schools-remarks/article_6c6c3a66-dd8b-11e9-b17b-f33f83a98daa.html

15 Medium.com https://medium.com/@kaimi.cambern/creating-a-dangerous-state-of-ha-wai%CA%BBi-governor-iges-press-conference-uh-prof-eae208c32976

16 UH Mānoa Department of Physics and Astronomy faculty members https://www.phys.hawaii.edu/faculty/

statues. Those street names need to be changed and those monuments and statues removed. Some examples include:

- Dole Street, Sanford B. Dole - Committee of Safety member

- Dole Food Company – started by James Dole, cousin of Sanford B. Dole, who came to Hawaiʻi five years after the overthrow, whose commercial activities would not have been possible without the annexation into the US[17]

- McKinley High School, named after William McKinley – the president who annexed Hawaiʻi into the US

- James B Castle High School, James' brother was William R Castle – Committee of Safety member

- Castle Street, William R Castle – Committee of Safety member

- Thurston Avenue, Lorrin A Thurston – Committee of Safety member

- Dillingham Boulevard, Benjamin F Dillingham – Committee of Safety member

- Atherton Road, Joseph B Atherton – Committee of Safety member

- Austin Road, Jonathan Austin – Committee of Safety member

- Bailey Road, William H Bailey – Committee of Safety member

They used shame as a powerful weapon of institutional racism. They made us feel shame, shame for our language, shame for our culture, and shame for the color of our non-white skin. They called us heathens who needed to be "saved." We were seen as

17 Wikipedia https://en.wikipedia.org/wiki/Dole_Food_Company#:~:text=James%20 Dole%2C%20who%20founded%20the,overthrow%20of%20the%20Hawaiian%20 monarchy.

primitive native savages who should be ashamed of ourselves. Shame is a powerful tool.

I wrote about that when I talked about my Tūtū shamed for speaking Hawaiian. They used shame culture and targeted the kānaka and the non-white local children. They shamed and beat the little ones in school. That's how they would get to the adults for speaking the Hawaiian language, through shaming their keiki. When the keiki grew up, they would carry that shame.

Hawai'i has carried that shame. As an island culture, locals still experience shame. It has a lot to do with living on a small island where in the past everybody's 'ohana was very connected to each other. We knew each other well and it seemed like everybody was "all up" in each other's business. The culture is changing today, but it still carries that shame.

We are different from the rest of the world because lodged within our local custom is the belief of not making waves or bringing shame to our 'ohana. So local people, in general, are not usually people who make noise or rebel. One of my college professors talked about teaching in Hawai'i and how different it is from the Continental US. She said that in schools there, hands go up everywhere and people talk, speak out, ask questions, agree, disagree and the like. She laughed and said, "Here, nobody talks or asks questions."

I thought to myself about the reason why locals are that way. One of the main reasons that I believe we are that way is because of the issue of shame. There are a few sayings like, "No make A/ Make A"* or "shame/no shame."* Those all have the root meaning of not wanting to be embarrassed. It is amplified in Hawai'i because we live on closely connected islands. If you have been around locals for any period of time, you have probably heard it.

"No make A" and "Make A" go together. "A" means "ass." The first means that a person does not want to make an ass of herself. The second means that one has made an ass of herself, and is expressing that she has done so and is probably feeling embarrassed because either somebody else has made fun of her, or she has embarrassed herself. "Shame" or "no shame" go together as well. "Shame" is more of a statement sometimes spoken to one's self as in, "Oh, shame. I forgot to bring food to the party." "No shame" is what somebody would say to another person. For example, "No shame, come eat. We get plenty food."

Let me give you an example since I've experienced it many times myself. Say I get invited to my friend's house. The local custom is that I always bring something, usually food to take over and give to them. Usually, I would stop off at Foodland grocery store and bring a ½ pound of poke* (raw fish) or some fried chicken from the deli. Bring something, that's a given. But what if I didn't have money that day, or didn't have time to stop off? Then when I get to my friend's house, I would apologize for not bringing anything. Usually, I feel shame because I came empty-handed. The shame would continue because his family would be eating or be in the process of having a meal. They would invite me to eat or offer me food. That is when the shame would show up like an invisible pareau* (sarong) wrapped around me. I would decline with some excuse because I didn't bring anything. So I would say, "oh nah das ok (no that's ok), I already ate," or "I not hungry, thanks" and they would insist that I eat. They would say, no shame (don't be embarrassed) in which case, I would eat something. I would always eat something even if I didn't want to or wasn't hungry because it is considered very rude to decline food that somebody's 'ohana offers. I would still feel a little shame, but it would eventually pass.

Now, if I forgot to bring food (it doesn't happen very often, I almost always bring something when I go to somebody's house) I would get a pass. My friend and his family would understand. But if it continues to happen, and I go over to their house all the time, and forget to bring something, or come empty-handed, then they would talk about me behind my back and not invite me back to their house because I "no more shame." That means that I don't have any shame and am a rude person. Worse yet, they would tell other people they know about me. That would reflect on me and my family especially if they told other people that I know about the situation. It would be shame if they told my 'ohana and word got around. It would seem like my family didn't teach me values growing up. Hawai'i is a small place.

Usually, non-locals get a pass. They are most times not familiar with our local customs. But once they've been here for a while, they are expected to pick it up, and eventually abide by it. If somebody continues to break that norm, local or non-local, they would be called "aku birds." Aku bird* is slang for a person who shows up to your house with nothing or barely anything to contribute, maybe bringing a bag of chips or a 6-pack of beer. He would eat all of his chips, drink all his beer, and then proceed to eat other people's food and drinks. The problem is, many times, nobody would confront the person and tell him that he is acting maha'oi* (rude, disrespectful) so the behavior would continue. Locals I know are usually bad at confronting others but good at talking behind their backs. That is my experience, and unfortunately, I have seen it and done it myself, so I am not bad-mouthing my local culture.

Shame is a mindset. In order to change, I have to change my thoughts and actions. I can change but it's easier said than done. I am saying it, and also doing my best to change that behavior in myself and teach my children too.

Another way to make change is to vote. This year, 2020, is an election year. In order to make change I will vote for candidates who share my values and beliefs, and hopefully, they get elected. I am tired of the status quo. The thing that encourages me the most, is seeing people take back their power. Power is in our hands. People are out in the streets protesting the symbols of racism. Confederate statues and statues representing men who were slave owners are being torn down everywhere. As I write, I can hear the people chanting, "Take it down! Take it down!" People have taken matters into their own hands. Like the statue of a confederate monument in North Carolina that was pulled down by protestors, people are doing things by themselves. They aren't waiting for the government to do the right thing. The people are doing the right thing. We, the people. Power to the people.

Glossary of Chapter 17

1. He – (HAY) the word for "a" or "an"
2. Kanaka – (KAH-NAH-KAH) a person, (usually) a man (see Chapter 9 for other definition)
3. No make A – Pidgin for don't make an "Ass" out of yourself, don't embarrass yourself
4. Make A – Pidgin for Make "Ass," meaning someone has made an ass of one's self
5. Shame – Pidgin for ashamed
6. No shame – Pidgin for don't be ashamed
7. Poke – (POH-KAY) raw fish, literally means cut into cubes or small pieces
8. Pareau – (PAH-DAY-OH) sarong dress, Tahitian word for a women's wrap-around garment

9. Aku bird – (AH-KOO) Pidgin for a person who habitually goes to parties, get-togethers etc., and barely contributes food or drink for others but eats or drinks from everyone else's supply

10. Maha'oi – (MA-HAH-OH-EEY) rude, behavior that is disrespectful or does not comply with local customs

CHAPTER 18

KA MĀKAʻI; THE POLICE

As I write this book, we are in a global Covid-19 pandemic and the Black Lives Matter Movement. Let me go on record to say, I support Black Lives Matter and want justice and equality for the poʻe pāʻele/haole (def #2) ʻeleʻele* (Black people), minorities, and all people of color.

Ka Mākaʻi* means the police. Here in Hawaiʻi, we have a unique situation and relationship with the mākaʻi. In a commentary by Trishia Kehaulani Watson, she explains her relationship with the police in Hawaiʻi:[1]

"I have never been afraid of the police here in Hawaii. Not once. And I realize now how that makes me not only fortunate – but privileged.

I have difficulty imagining a life in which the police are feared. I cannot even begin to understand living in a community where the police are not a resource in dangerous situations. While I have certainly been subject to racism and racial profiling on the US continent, I've never worried that I would be physically harmed by law enforcement as a result of that racism. It's from that place of privilege that I view the "defund the police" movement.

---

1   Civil Beat https://www.civilbeat.org/2020/06/trisha-kehaulani-watson-struggling-to-make-sense-of-calls-to-defund-the-police/

While I do not doubt that bad actors exist in any institution, I personally feel our police force here in Hawaii does not categorically have the same institutionalized issues with racism that other departments across the United States do.

I can't help but wonder if this is due in part to the fact that the racial composition of our police force closely mirrors the diversity of our residents. In fact, an article from the Bookings Institute on "Minority under-representation in city and suburban policing" showed that minorities were over-represented in Honolulu, with minorities comprising 86.7 percent of the Honolulu Police Department compared to the island's population, which is 80.6 percent minority.

I don't know many local people, particularly in the Hawaiian community, who don't have relatives on the police force. I have a cousin who is a great police officer. I'm incredibly proud of him."

There is one incident with law enforcement that rocked Hawai'i. That was the case of Kollin Elderts. On November 5, 2011, at approximately 2:30 a.m., Elderts crossed paths with a US Diplomatic Security Service Special Agent, Christopher Deedy, a haole (def#1 & #2) from Arlington, Virginia, at a McDonald's in Waikīkī. It was there that they got into an argument and then a fight in which Deedy used deadly force against the unarmed local native Hawaiian man, Elderts. Deedy fired 3 shots from his Glock 9mm handgun. Two shots missed, and 1 hit Elderts in his chest, collapsing his lung and killing him.

Like the case with Rayshard Brooks at a Wendy's in Atlanta, Georgia on June 12, 2020, where Brooks was shot in the back and killed by police, was deadly force on the part of law enforcement necessary? According to law professor Ken Lawson in his explanation of when deadly force may be used, he explains,[2] "deadly

---

2   YouTube "Police shooting of Rayshard Brooks, Professor Ken Lawson" https://www. youtube.com/watch?v=aJCV9yTRhGA

force may only be used when necessary to avoid being the victim of deadly force; or when the other actor's use of deadly force is imminent." In explaining how much force may be used, he says that the officer,[3] "may only use as much force as is necessary to avoid being the victim of deadly force."

Let's look at the facts in the Kollin Elderts and Christopher Deedy case explained in the Offshore podcast[4] and security camera footage[5] on the night of the killing:

1. Earlier that night Deedy's haole (def#1 & #2) friend Agent Finklestein warns Deedy about locals. He says that "some Hawaiians don't like outsiders, or haoles (def#1 & #2)." Deedy decides based on that warning to carry his firearm while off-duty for a night of partying and drinking. He goes out with friends where they party and drink. Deedy later testifies that he had only had about 4 drinks over a 6 hour time period even though his credit card records indicate that he had ordered lots of drinks that night.

2. Earlier that night Kollin Elderts, a local native Hawaiian man also was out with his friends drinking, smoking pot, and partying. He is from Kailua, Oʻahu and is celebrating with friends and spending the night at a hotel in Waikīkī.

3. At about 2:30 a.m. on November 5, 2011 Deedy and his friends Jessica West and Adam Gutowski all end up in a Waikīkī McDonald's to get a late-night snack. They order their food and go sit down.

4. About 10 minutes later, both Elderts and his friend Shane Medeiros enter and order food. Elderts had words with a man

---

3   Ibid #91

4   Offshore Podcast Season 1: A Killing in Waikiki https://www.offshorepodcast.org/

5   YouTube "Deedy trial video from McDonald's Security Camera" https://www.youtube.com/watch?v=K_CDhTH_EgE&t=1435s

named Michel Perrine. Elderts was calling Perrine names and teasing him, calling him haole (def#1).

5. Deedy walked over to Elderts. Deedy claimed that he was trying to prevent an altercation between Elderts and Perrine. A female McDonald's security worker came over to see what was happening but Deedy never identified himself as a law enforcement agent to her.

6. Elderts and Deedy have angry words against each other and Deedy got angry. Their friends try and keep them apart and step away from each other.

7. Medeiros and Gutowski start fighting with each other.

8. Minutes later Elderts and Deedy begin fighting. Then Deedy shoots Elderts (off-camera). Kollin Eldert's lung collapsed. Deedy killed him.

Deedy was arrested and the case went to trial. He was tried for 2nd-degree murder. The first trial resulted in a hung jury. He was retried again and in the second trial, Deedy was found not guilty of 2nd-degree murder. The jury was hung on manslaughter and assault charges. Almost 9 years after he killed Kollin Elderts, the US Supreme Court ruled in June 2020 that they won't hear the case on whether Deedy should be tried a third time. Acting Prosecuting Attorney, Dwight Nadamoto said, "the circumstances in which Christopher Deedy killed Kollin Elderts are similar to recent killings on the mainland that have sparked worldwide outrage… Deedy was a law enforcement officer who needlessly escalated an encounter with an unarmed citizen in the unjustified use of lethal force."[6]

Christopher Deedy's Facebook community page was last updated in 2015. It showed that he was still employed as a US

---

6   Federal News Network https://federalnewsnetwork.com/government-news/2020/06/high-court-wont-hear-federal-agents-hawaii-shooting-case/

Federal Agent. [7] As Deedy remains free today, these questions come to my mind:

> Question #1: In the wake of the Black Lives Matter movement, would it be right to revisit this case to prove or disprove whether race was a factor when Deedy killed Elderts? Deedy decided to carry his concealed firearm based on his friend's warning that some locals don't like "haoles (def#1 & #2)." Elderts and Medeiros were heard calling Perrine and Deedy "haoles" (def#1) before the fighting started at McDonald's on the night of the killing.
>
> Question #2: Did Deedy use deadly force on the night of the killing? Elderts and Medeiros were both unarmed men. Deedy was the only person who was armed with a gun, even though he was off duty, and had been drinking.
>
> Question #3: Should law enforcement agents be allowed to carry handguns while consuming alcohol (or any mind-altering substance)? In both 2015 & 2016, the Hawai'i House Bill #1129 in honor of Kollin Elderts, was introduced into the legislature to "prohibit law enforcement officers from consuming any amount of alcohol while in the possession on their person or control of a firearm." [8] Both times, the bill died.

My younger daughter, Hi'ilani, told me something last week that bothered me and got me thinking. She said, "Mommy, I'm scared of the police." Instead of listening to her, I tried to protect her. "It is

7   Facebook https://www.facebook.com/deedysupport

8   LegiScan https://legiscan.com/HI/research/HB1129/2015

scary with everything that is going on right now'" I told her, "don't be scared, we don't have to be scared of them." But was I right to say that she doesn't need to be afraid of them? She is relatively safe in Hawai'i. That's true because she's a local girl. But she's a DARK brown local girl. What if she went to the US Continent? She could be mistaken for a black girl if she went there. What then? Is it still right to say she doesn't need to be afraid of them?

I can relate to Trisha Kehaulani Watson's experiences, as mine were similar. I was never afraid of the police growing up. They were and still are our friends and relatives. My mom played softball with a lady cop that we called, Aunty Belinda. My dad played on a team with his detective friend, Uncle Gilbert. After high school, many of my classmates and even my ex-boyfriend went on to join the police department.

I was safe and protected by the police until the conflict on Maunakea started. It instilled fear, mistrust, and anger in me against the police. That issue continues to make me wary of the police. The TMT organization is still pushing to get their way and spending lots of money to persuade people to see them favorably. They are using their money to run pro-TMT commercials and propaganda. They have the backing of the State of Hawai'i and its resources, including the police force.

The first time I went up to Maunakea in September 2019, I felt very tense. I noticed a lot of police near the surrounding areas. I saw two makeshift police camps on my way up and another one that was set up right across the road from the restrooms at the Maunakea State Park with officers sitting in their police cars watching people exit and enter the park area.

Up to that point, I had never been the target of racial profiling. Racial profiling is "the discriminatory practice by law enforcement officials of targeting individuals for suspicion of crime based on the individual's race, ethnicity, religion, or national origin."[9]

Several weeks later, one early Saturday morning on Oʻahu, I was driving from my apartment to my daughters' dad's house in Mililani. It was their week with him, so I was going to pick something up from them at his house. As I was driving on Kamehameha Highway passing Mililani Shopping Center, I noticed a cop car coming up the hill behind me. I didn't pay attention, because I didn't have reason to. I was driving the speed limit and my car's paperwork was up to date (registration, insurance, safety check) so I had no reason for concern. Then as I was getting into the left lane to turn up Meheʻula Parkway, the cop cut in and was right behind me. I waited, turned left at the light, and then turned right to go down past Nob Hill. The cop turned and followed me again.

That's when I got nervous. I was thinking about my safety check, insurance, registration, and license. I said to myself, "What the hell? Is this cop following me? What for? I have a white 4 door compact Honda mom-car with a Disneyland license plate holder. I'm a law-abiding citizen. Shit, the cop must be racial profiling me because of my sticker!" That's when I got really scared, my hands and body started shaking, but I was mad. I was thinking about how we were smack in the middle of the Maunakea movement and I had a 5x7" "We are Maunakea" sticker that I bought from my friend, Kanoa Dahlin's company @h_icon808, on the left rear windshield.

Hawaiian culture is my #1 value. I hold it up high, right next to my hae Hawaiʻi* (Hawaiian flag) on my bedroom wall. My culture is near and dear to my heart. If you push up against my Hawaiian cultural values, I will stand up to you, and I will be fricken pissed if I feel you are disrespecting that.

---

9   ACLU https://www.aclu.org/other/racial-profiling-definition

I don't swear a lot around other people (more about swear words in the next chapter). But that day I lost it. I figured that the "WE ARE MAUNAKEA" sticker was the reason I was being followed, AND because I was in Mililani, an upper-middle-class city. I lost it when the cop turned right and followed me onto the street where my kids live.

I was driving and talking out loud as if I was talking to the cop. I was getting ready to give her a piece of my mind. "Brah* (Pidgin slang word)," I said. I turned into the driveway of my kids' house and pressed the remote garage door opener hanging from my car window shade so the cop would know that I belonged there. I put my car in park and jumped out of my car. Door open, car running, body shaking.

When I get super-pissed, my body or my hands start shaking, and I sometimes cry, like the Denzel Washington one tear cry, but out of both eyes. I give a mean stink eye* too, full-on intense. I felt my heart beating inside my body. It sounded like my whole body was beating because my body was shaking with fear.

I was standing on the edge of the driveway on the sidewalk right next to the neighbor's white fence. It was a lady cop. She had her window up and looked like she was in her late 30s, early 40s. She was dark-skinned, maybe part Hawaiian, Polynesian. She was a local chick, black hair pulled back in a tight bun, and wearing shades. She stopped and slowly began turning her police car around in front of the next-door neighbor's house. She had her shades on but didn't turn toward me or make eye contact with me as the police car made a U-turn. I lost it. My body was shaking, my hands were clenched, and I was sweating. Even though her window was up and she couldn't hear me, she could tell by my body language that I was pissed I took off my shades and as I watched her turn, I had my chest pushed out, and was gesturing with my hands in my "what, what" (hands open in the "You want a piece of me?") stance. She could read my lips if she tried, cause I was yelling. She was looking straight ahead not once turning her face in my direction. I said, "WAT FAKA? I NOT SKEDA YOU. YOU FUCKEN RACIAL PROFILING ME? HAH? YOU TINK I NO LIVE OVA HEA? HAH? YOU TINK I ONE POOR HAWAIIAN? FAKA WAT (What fucker? I am not afraid of you. Are you fucking racial profiling me? Huh? You think that I don't live here? Huh? You think that I'm a poor Hawaiian? Fucker what)?"

Glossary of Chapter 18

1. Poʻe Pāʻele – (POH-AY-PAH-EH-LAY) Black People
2. Haole ʻeleʻele – (HOW-LAY-EH-LAY-EH-LAY) Negroes, literally means Black foreigners (def#2)
3. Ka mākaʻi – (KAH-MA-KAH-EEY) the police
4. Hae Hawaiʻi – (HA-EH-HAH-WAH-EEY) Hawaiian flag
5. Brah – Pidgin slang word sometimes meaning brother, usually said to a male
6. Stink eye – Pidgin for the evil eye, staring somebody down

CHAPTER 19

NĀ ʻŌLELO PELAPELA; SWEAR WORDS, "UNACCEPTABLE" LANGUAGE

Swear words or curse words are considered by most as "unacceptable" language and "defined as profanity: vulgar, socially unacceptable language you don't use in polite conversation."[1] The word pelapela* means obscene or nasty. Nā ʻōlelo pelapela means "the swear words" or "the obscene/nasty words." There are no swear words in Hawaiian that are equivalent to the English words "fuck" or "shit." Based on my understanding of the Hawaiian language (my opinion only), I would say that words were valuable since words were spoken and not written. Words were held in high regard in the way it was passed down orally through chants, etc. Only the most necessary words were probably spoken and passed down.

Take for example "The Kumulipo,"[2] i Hawaiian creation chant with 2,102 lines and 16 chants. Now imagine being the person or persons responsible for memorizing all 2,102 lines. If I were

---

1   New York Times https://www.nytimes.com/2017/07/27/smarter-living/the-case-for-cursing.html

2   Beckwith, The Kumulipo a Hawaiian Creation Chant

responsible for holding all of those lines in my memory, I would want only the most essential words. It would be my responsibility to make sure I pass it on accurately to the next generation.

Imagine that you had 16 grown adult kids who were all married. Each couple had 10 kids. Now imagine you have to retell each couple's story and remember at least 6 facts about each person. That would include important details of each couple's story, like wedding days, birthdays, where their children were born, how each of their children got their names or the meaning of their names, and where they live. Now add to memory each person's cell phone number (16 kids + 16 spouses + 10 kids per couple = 320 people x 6.57 facts per person = 2,102). That is a lot to memorize. I know I couldn't do it.

Just because Hawaiians didn't have swear words doesn't mean they didn't say negative things or use bad words against others. It just meant that they were more careful with the words that they spoke. They used epithets to cut down a certain person, talk about his character, family, or place that he lived in. For example:[3]

Lazy Person: *'Ōlelo No'eau 121: "A nui mai ke kai o Waialua, moe pupu'u o Kalena i Hale 'au'au." Applied to a person who prefers to sleep instead of doing chores. A play on lena (lazy), in Kalena, who was a fisherman, and hale (house) in Hale 'au'au.*

Ungrateful person: 'Ōlelo No'eau 85: "'Ai no ka 'iole a ha'alele i kona kūkae." A rat eats, then leaves its droppings, said of an ungrateful person.

Unfriendly people: 'Ōlelo No'eau 2354: "O'ahu maka 'ewa'ewa." O'ahu of the averted eyes. This saying began with Hi'iaka, who asked two of her kinsmen on O'ahu for a canoe to take her to Kaua'i. They gave her a broken one, which she and her companion mended with no help from the men. In disgust, she

---

3   Puku'l, 'Ōlelo No'eau Book

called them Oʻahu maka ʻewaʻewa. After that, Oʻahu was said to have the least friendly people of all the islands.

Pidgin was another form of language that was deemed "unacceptable." In 1987, the Board of Education banned Pidgin from the classroom. One argument they used was that "HCE (Hawaiian Creole English) fosters illiteracy."[4] Local people were angry and argued that "HCE was a vital aspect of local identity. Learning SAE (Standard American English) does not mean having to relinquish HCE. Teachers rejected the policy with lack of participation. The Department of Education was asked to develop a language arts program for HCE speaking students and look into the possibility of obtaining federal funds for such programs."[5]

In 1999, Pidgin was blamed for the low English scores of Hawaiʻi's students. School leaders said that it was because Hawaiʻi students did poorly on a national writing test. They blamed it on Pidgin even though they had no evidence to validate that claim. In September 1999, "the National Assessment of Educational Progress found that only 72 percent of island eighth-graders were writing at or above basic achievement levels, compared with 83 percent nationwide. It also found that only 15 percent of the students were at or above proficiency levels, compared with 24 percent nationally."[6] However, Hawaiʻi's student scores consistently rank lower than the national average.[7]

Former Hawaiʻi Board of Education chairman Mitsugi Nakashima said, "If your thinking is not in standard English, it's hard for you to write in standard English… We ought to have classrooms where standard English is the norm rather than teachers

4   Studyblue https://www.studyblue.com/notes/note/n/hawaiian-creole-english/deck/14436741

5   Ibid #4

6   Deseret News "Pidgin English blamed for low test scores" https://www.deseret.com/1999/11/27/19477564/pidgin-english-blamed-for-low-scores

7   Ibid #6

having to use pidgin English to get points across.."[8] Former Hawai'i Superintendent of Education Paul LeMahieu said, "Students should not be discouraged from speaking pidgin, but rather should learn to use different dialects in different settings."[9] Former Hawai'i Governor Ben Cayetano, "who admits occasionally lapsing into pidgin, sees no reason for using it in classrooms when students face a world ruled by "the king's English."[10]

Pidgin advocates have a different perspective. They say, "that efforts to stamp out the language from school settings is simply discrimination in disguise."[11] Pidgin Coup member and UH Mānoa *Ph*.D. student whose focus includes Hawai'i Creole sociolinguistics, Gavin Furukawa says, "It's a type of racism and language is just an excuse for it."[12]

According to the Nation's Report card, the most current data for reading showed:[13]

**O-lowest score   500-highest score

Year	Grade	Hawai'i English Scores**	English National Average**
4th graders			
1998	4th	200	215/213
2000	4th	-	215/211

---

8   Ibid #6

9   Ibid #6

10 Ibid #6

11 Civil Beat https://www.civilbeat.org/2013/03/18498-fo-teach-pidgin-o-not-fo-teach-pidgin-das-da-question/

12 Ibid #11

13 The Nation's Report Card https://www.nationsreportcard.gov/profiles/stateprofile/overview/HI?cti=PgTab_OT&chort=1&sub=MAT&sj=HI&fs=Grade&st=MN&year=2019R3&sg=Gender%3A+Male+vs.+Female&sgv=Difference&ts=Single+-Year&tss=2019R3-2019R3&sfj=NP

2002	4th	208	217
2003	4th	208	216
2005	4th	210	217
2007	4th	213	220
2009	4th	211	220
2011	4th	214	220
2013	4th	215	221
2015	4th	215	221
2017	4th	216	221
2019	4th	218	219
8th graders			
1998	8th	250/249	250
2000	8th	-	-
2002	8th	252	263
2003	8th	251	261
2005	8th	249	260
2007	8th	251	261
2009	8th	255	262
2011	8th	257	264
2013	8th	260	266
2015	8th	257	264
2017	8th	261	265
2019	8th	258	262

Based on the data, there is a significant jump in Hawai'i Students' 4th grade English scores from 1998-2002. Since no data was collected in 1999, the year they tried to implement Standard English only, it cannot be determined whether discouraging Pidgin was the cause of the increase.

Based on the data from 1998-2007 for 8th grade English, scores remained relatively the same. Scores ranged between 249-251 during those years, showing no significant improvement after 1999. Therefore based on the data, Pidgin did not seem to have any effect on test scores for 8th graders in those 9-years.

The overall data is not accurate because #1 data was not collected to chart and monitor students' progress of those who regularly spoke Pidgin at home. There was no way to confirm whether the scores from students who spoke Pidgin went up because the data for all students (Pidgin and non-Pidgin speakers) were lumped together; #2 Standardized tests are inherently racially biased. "These tests are often designed with racial, cultural, and socio-economic bias built in."[14]

Society stereotypes some accents, and ways of speaking as "low class." Other accents are perceived as "high class." What stereotypes come to mind when you hear Pidgin? Southern Drawl? Boston accent? How about the British accent? Australian accent? Black English/African-American vernacular English? One of the reasons why I love Tiffany Haddish is because she speaks black English. She is so funny and cracks me up!

Swear words are interesting to me. I never swore a lot growing up, maybe its because my female role models like my mom did not swear. As a teacher, I used to have a rule of no swearing. I used to get offended when I heard the students swearing, but not so much anymore. I became a "closet car swearer" a couple of years ago,

14 Next Gen Learning https://www.nextgenlearning.org/articles/racial-bias-standard-ized-testing

and it actually makes me feel better. I define myself as a closet car swearer because I mostly swear when I am alone, or driving in my car. I swear when another driver does something dangerous or stupid. I also swear when I am extremely happy, lol.

My opinion about Pidgin and swearing changed a few years ago. I used to think a lot about it when I would tell kids not to swear in my class. I still tell them to watch their language, but I give them reminders, instead of punishing or making them feel bad. I don't say stuff like, "Somebody should wash your mouth out with soap," or "You know how stupid you sound?" I think about the man who came to Uncle Bud's office. He felt comfortable after my mom started talking Pidgin to him. I think about kids whose parents and adult loved ones swear or talk Pidgin all the time. How would that affect them or their opinions of their loved ones if I said, "only uneducated people talk Pidgin or swear," or "people who swear or talk Pidgin are low class." I would be talking stink* (bad-mouthing) about their loved ones.

I vowed to myself to never speak negatively or degrade people who talk Pidgin or swear, here's why. One day at school during lunchtime, I was talking story with a student. He was a local haole (def#1) boy who spoke Pidgin and swore, A LOT in class. I wanted to get an idea as to why he swore so much in my class, and also get to know him a little better. We were talking story about his hobbies. Here's how our conversation went, I'll call him Jeff:

Jeff: Ho Kumu, I love fo fish. Me an my dad we go errytime togedah (Whoah, Kumu, I love to fish. Me and my dad we go every time together).

Me: O wow, how offen you guys go (Oh wow, how often you guys go)?

Jeff: Yah, we go whenevahs. We facken love fo fish, brah (Yeah, we go whenever. We fucking love to fish, brah).

Me: Ok. So jus you an yo fadah? You guys close (Ok. So just you and your dad? You guys are close)?

Jeff: Fak yah. We real close (Fuck yeah. We are really close).

Me: Wow, he muss be one real good faddah (Wow, he must be a really good dad).

Jeff: He solid. But he give me cracks wen he get mad, but das how he teach me (He's good. But he wacks me when he's angry, but that's how he teaches me).

Me: He buss you up (He beats you)?

Jeff: Nah Kumu. He one good dad. He juss get mad wen I do stoopid kine stuffs. He mossly jus sweah at me wen I ack like one dummy (No Kumu. He's a good dad. He just gets angry when I do stupid things. He mostly just swears at me when I act foolishly).

Me: Ok, ok. Juss makin shua dat you ok (Ok, ok. Just making sure that you're ok).

Jeff: He teach me planny stuffs, spechally fishin lai-dat. Brah, we fish togedah all da taim (He teaches me a lot of things, especially fishing like that. Brah, we fish together all the time).

Me: I can ass you one question (Can I ask you a question)?

Jeff: Yah, shua (Yes, sure).

Me: You tink sweareen ok? Like if adults sweah wen dey arounn deh kids (You think swearing is ok? Like if adults swear when they are around their kids)?

Jeff: Yah. Das how me ann my fadah talk to each ahddah. He sweah planny and das jus how he ack. He sweah when he mad, he sweah when he not mad. Das jus him. He talk Pidgin too, das why I talk lai-dis (Yeah. That's how me and my father talk to each other. He swears a lot and that's just how he acts. He swears when he's angry, he swears when he's not angry. That's just him. He talks Pidgin too, that's why I talk like this).

Me: Right on. Natting wrong wit dat, brah. So das why you sweah so much in my class den [smile], yah (Right on. Nothing's wrong with that, brah. So that's why you swear so much in my class then, yeah)?

Jeff: Yah, Kumu. I sorry. No can help das why. Not tryinna disrespeck you (Yeah, Kumu. Sorry. I can't help it that's why. Not trying to disrespect you).

Me: Nah, all good [laugh]. I undahstan (No problem, it's all good. I understand).

Statistics mean nothing until you see its effects on the real lives of real people. It makes me sad because I hardly hear young people talking Pidgin. As a high school kumu, I hear a lot of things, and I hardly hear Pidgin. It is dying. In the article by Civil Beat, "Educators: Pidgin Belongs in Hawaii Schools," Doreen Tabe, a

Waimalu Elementary School Librarian said, "she personally feels the language is dying among youths, based on her observations. Tabe grew up in Hawaii, but also lived in California and attended school in Chicago. She said using Pidgin on the mainland was something 'I always tried to hide, I was really self-conscious about it."[15]

I talk Pidgin all the time in class. It makes me feel comfortable, and it seems to make my students feel comfortable with me too. I get the vibe that my students feel like I'm somebody they can talk to when I break out and talk Pidgin on the first day of school. It seems to loosen them up because they can see that I'm not some stuffy, uppity "proper" English talking kumu. I think they see me as a down to earth person they can relate to.

I had a really funny Pidgin experience with one of my haole (def#1) girl students. When she came into my class, she looked down and acted very nervous during the first few weeks. She never looked at me or smiled. I didn't know if she was afraid of me, or that was just her personality. She spoke standard English and didn't interact too much with the other kids. After a couple of weeks, she kind of warmed up to me. One day, I walked around the classroom while they were broken up into groups. She was practicing a chord on the ʻukulele and had a hard time putting her fingers on the frets to get the right sound. I told her, "holem lai-dis and pucho fingah ova-hea to get one taita grip so soun good addawaiz goin soun flat (hold ʻem like this and put your finger over here to get a tighter grip so it sounds good otherwise it's going to sound flat)." So she did what I said and got the right grip. She strummed the chord, and it sounded right on. Then she leaned over to one of the girls on her table and said, "Kumu said, lai-dis," and they both laughed. I turned around to them and said, "Das right, sistah (that's right,

15 Civil Beat https://www.civilbeat.org/2017/10/pidgin-belongs-in-hawaii-schools-educators-say/

sister). Lai-dis means like this and lai-dat means like that." The three of us started laughing and then I walked away. Maybe it was the Pidgin, maybe it was laughing together, maybe it was both. I felt a real connection with her after that day.

Glossary of Chapter 19

1. Pelapela – (PEH-LAH-PEH-LAH) Obscene, filthy, lewd, nasty

2. Nā ʻōlelo pelapela – (NAH-OH-LEH-LOW-PEH-LAH-PEH-LAH) the swear words, the curse words [plural]

3. Talk stink – Pidgin for talking bad about someone, bad-mouthing another person

CHAPTER 20

KE ALAULA; A NEW BEGINNING

Ke alaula* literally means the flaming road. It also means the flash of light right before the sun rises, and the flash right before the sun sets. It signifies the cyclical nature of life. Everything in creation has a beginning and an end.

A pono* (righteous) beginning and ending encompass liberty and justice as in, "The Pledge of Allegiance," statement "With liberty and justice for all." Liberty according to Webster means, "the quality or state of being free."[1] Justice is defined as, "the use of authority and power to uphold what is right, just, or lawful."[2]

An apology is a good first step. It's a beginning. In 1993, US President Bill Clinton signed the "Apology Resolution," acknowledging America's role in the overthrow:[3] "Public Law 103-50, to acknowledge the 100 anniversary of the January 17, 1893 overthrow of the Kingdom of Hawaii, and to offer apology to Native Hawaiians on behalf of the United States for the overthrow of the Kingdom of Hawaii."

---

1   Merriam-Webster https://www.merriam-webster.com/dictionary/liberty

2   Collins https://www.collinsdictionary.com/us/dictionary/english/justice

3   Capitol https://www.capitol.hawaii.gov/session1999/bills/HR201_.htm

Where do Hawaiians go next? The Hawaiʻi state motto spoken by King Kamehameha III-Kauikeaouli* gives clear direction. The motto is, "Ua mau ke <u>ea</u> o ka ʻāina i ka pono"* (the sovereignty of the land is perpetuated in righteousness). An article in the Kaʻiwakīloumoku explains "ea"* (sovereignty):[4]

"If your ʻhanabata daysʻ were spent in public school classrooms, you probably recognize this saying as the motto of the State of Hawaiʻi, and have heard its most common translation, ʻthe life of the land is perpetuated in righteousness.ʻ This is one possible meaning of the saying, yet it makes no reference to the original sentiment that makes the saying so memorable. The words ʻUa mau ke ea o ka ʻāina i ka ponoʻ were first uttered by Kamehameha III on July 31, 1843. He was addressing his people after independence was restored to the Kingdom of Hawaiʻi following five months of British occupation. Given the circumstances, perhaps a better interpretation of the saying would be ʻThe sovereignty of the land is perpetuated through justice.ʻ Yet a slightly different analysis of the word ʻponoʻ to mean universal balance and harmony, also offers a holistic explanation: ʻThe life or sovereignty of the land is maintained in harmony.ʻ It is our hope that all people have access to and apply their own ancestral wisdom to guide them through times of difficulties and hardships. And that in the end, justice and harmony will prevail."

Another explanation is given by kumu Umi Perkins in his Ted Talks video:[5]

"Speaking of the State of Hawaiʻi, we all know the motto of the State of Hawaiʻi, ʻUa mau ke ea o ka ʻāina i ka ponoʻ and we're told that it means ʻthe life of the land is perpetuated in righteousness.ʻ But if you look at the context in which that... it was

---

4   Kaʻiwakīloumoku https://apps.ksbe.edu/kaiwakiloumoku/uamaukeeaokaainaikapono

5   YouTube "Ted Talks Umi Perkins" https://www.youtube.com/watch?v=TVsk1O8KM-BI&t=786s

originally stated, it wasn't a poem. It was... well you know, my students know about the band 'Sudden Rush,' that rap group who say, "Hawaiians tell me what you want, ea." Life? No. Sovereignty. The sovereignty of the land is perpetuated in righteousness. So on the state seal emblazoned in large print is a sovereignty slogan for the Hawaiian Kingdom that says that sovereignty is perpetuated. It continues. In other words the motto of the state of Hawai'i denies the existence of the State of Hawai'i."

Lyrics from the chorus of the song "Ea" by the popular rap group "Sudden Rush:"[6]

(Rapper Don Ke'ala Kawa'auhau Jr.)

Ea – chorus

To all my people tell me what you want EA

Hawaiians tell me what you need EA

Trying to take what the kānaka maoli got EA

Just to satisfy the government's greed 'A'OLE

Hawaiians tell me what you want EA

Kānaka maoli tell me what you need EA

We must never forget what our kūpuna taught

EA even if I have to bleed

I see the flaming road as my life's path. It is the path that I walk, as everyone is responsible to walk their own path that has been set before them. I remember the bright flash of light that announced

---

6   YouTube "Sudden Rush Ea" https://www.youtube.com/watch?v=hgmOO5jiiq0

my arrival on this earth. I know this trip is short. I'll never forget that there will be another bright flash of light that will declare my departure from this honua* (earth). It will be the stunning flash that marks the next journey of my life into the next world.

The flash at the start of my life was the flash that signified the start of the race. My race. "On your mark, get set, GO!" My ancestors lit my torch and passed it on to me to lead and to guide me. The kukui* (light) guides me with warmth and wisdom for my travels. It is their stories and their lives. The more pages I add to my moʻolelo, my story, by teaching others and giving guidance, the brighter it burns. I must protect it from anything that tries to extinguish it.

Mahalo to you who caused my kukui to burn brighter. Mahalo to you who fanned the flame of my kukui when it was on the verge of burning out. Mahalo to you who watched and protected my kukui when I didn't, couldn't, or wouldn't. Mahalo to you for showing me how so I can show the next generation too: my kids, nieces, nephews, students, and anyone else that I can mālama. Mahalo to you, the reader, for spending time to holoholo with me on this huakaʻi.

Until we meet again, a hui hou*...

Glossary of Chapter 20

1. Alaula – (AH-LAH-OOH-LAH) light of early dawn, the flaming road

2. Pono – (POH-NOH) moral, upright, just

3. Kauikeaouli – (KAH-OOH-EEY-KEH-OW-OOH-LEE) King Kamehameha III, third king of the Kingdom of Hawaiʻi

4. Ua mau ke ea o ka ʻāina i ka pono (OOH-AH-MA-OOH-KEH-EH-AH-OH-KAH-AYE-NAH-EEY-KAH-POH-NOH) State motto of Hawaiʻi in which they translate it to mean "the <u>life</u>

170

of the land is perpetuated in righteousness" is an incorrect translation. The more appropriate translation is "the <u>sovereignty</u> of the land is perpetuated in righteousness"

5. Ea – (EH-AH) sovereignty

6. Honua – (HOE-NOO-AH) earth, land

7. Kukui – KOO-KOO-EEY) light, lamp, candle, candlenut tree

8. A hui hou (AH-WHO-EEY-HOE) – until we meet again